HOW TO PERFORM

HAJJ & UMRAH

HOW TO PERFORM
HAJJ & UMRAH

According to the Four Sunni Schools of Law

SHAYKH NŪR AL-DĪN ʿITR

Translated by

AMJAD MAHMOOD

HERITAGE
PRESS

How to Perform Hajj and Umrah According to the Four Sunni Schools of Law

Published by: Heritage Press
Published in: September 2013/Shawwāl 1434 H
Reprinted in: July 2015/Ramadan 1436 H
Website: www.heritagepress.co.uk
E-mail: info@heritagepress.co.uk

Author: Shaykh Nūr al-Dīn ʿItr
Translation: Amjad Mahmood

A catalogue record of this book is available from the British Library.

ISBN: 978-0-9576937-1-5

Typeset by: N.A. Qaddoura
Cover design by: Mohammad Almass, www.studioalmass.com
Printed in Turkey by: Imak Ofset

Contents

Transliteration key x
Translator's introduction xi
Shaykh Nūr al-Dīn 'Itr xv
Author's introduction 1

1: The Fundamental Rulings of Hajj 3
The obligation to perform hajj and its pre-requisites 3
Hastening to perform hajj 4
The conditions for the obligation to perform hajj 5
The conditions for the validity of hajj 8
Things which are unlawful in *iḥrām* 13
1. Things unlawful for one to wear 13
An important clarification for men regarding the ruling of tying the upper and lower garment 15
2. Unlawful matters pertaining to the body of someone in *iḥrām* 16
Applying perfume 18
3. Hunting 20
4. Sexual intercourse and foreplay 21

5. Acts of impiety (*fisq*) and disputation 22
Things which are lawful in *iḥrām* 22
The integrals of hajj 23
The necessary acts (*wājibāt*) in hajj 24
1. Regarding the *iḥrām* 25
2. Regarding the *ṭawāf* 25
3. Necessary acts during the standing in ʿArafah 26
4. Necessary acts in Minā 27
The sunnahs of hajj 28
The fundamental sunnahs of hajj 29

2: The Fundamental Rulings of Umrah 31
The obligatory acts in umrah 31
The necessary acts in umrah 32
Iḥrām for umrah 32

3: The Various Methods of Performing Hajj and Their Legality 34
The method of *al-tamattuʿ* 35
The method of *al-qirān* 35
The sacrificial offering for the completion of *al-tamattuʿ* and *al-qirān* 36
The time of the sacrificial offering for *al-qirān* and *al-tamattuʿ* 37
The place in which the sacrifice is offered by a *qārin* or a *mutamattiʿ* 37
The validity of the three methods of hajj 38
Which of these types of pilgrimage is best? 40
Important notice regarding the hajj of a woman during menses and lochia 41

4: The Method of Performing Hajj and Umrah and Their Transmitted Supplications 44
Preparation for the journey to perform hajj or umrah 45
Recommendations for the journey and its supplications 46
Dispensations for a traveller 48
Necessary guidelines for safety 50
How to perform umrah and its supplications 51
Entering Mecca 56
Entering the Sacred Mosque 58
circumambulation (*Ṭawāf*) 60
The supplications for *ṭawāf* 63
The first cycle of the *ṭawāf* 65
The second cycle of the *ṭawāf* 66
The third cycle of the *ṭawāf* 68
The fourth cycle of the *ṭawāf* 69
The fifth cycle of the *ṭawāf* 71
The sixth cycle of the *ṭawāf* 72
The seventh cycle of the *ṭawāf* 73
The prayer after the *ṭawāf* and its supplication 75
The supplication when drinking Zamzam 76
The supplication at the *Multazam* 77
The walk (*saʿy*) between al-Ṣafā and al-Marwah 78
The supplications during the cycle of *saʿy* 82
The first cycle of the *saʿy* 82
The second cycle of the *saʿy* 83
The third cycle of the *saʿy* 84
The fourth cycle of the *saʿy* 86
The fifth cycle of the *saʿy* 88

The sixth cycle of the *saʿy* 89
The seventh cycle of the *saʿy* 91
Release from the state of *iḥrām* for a *mutamattiʿ* pilgrim and the one performing umrah only 93
The *mufrid* and the *qārin* 94
Staying in Mecca 94
Entering the revered Kaaba 95
How to perform hajj and its supplications 96
The daily rites of hajj 99
The Day of *Tarwiyah* 99
The Day of ʿArafah 101
Proceeding towards ʿArafah 101
The supplications in ʿArafah 103
Setting off for al-Muzdalifah and spending the night therein 117
Standing in al-Muzdalifah 119
The supplications in al-Muzdalifah 119
Picking up the stones 121
Travelling towards Minā 121
The Day of Sacrifice 122
The rituals in Minā on the Day of Sacrifice 122
Stoning the ʿAqabah Site (*Jamrah al-ʿAqabah*) 123
The sacrifice 125
Shaving or shortening the hair 126
The *Ṭawāf* of the Visit (*Ṭawāf al-Ziyārah*) [also known as the *Ṭawāf* of Departure (*Ṭawāf al-Ifāḍah*)] 128
The first release from *iḥrām* (*al-taḥallul al-awwal*) 129
The second release from *iḥrām* (*al-taḥallul*

al-thānī) 129
The first and second days of *al-Tashrīq* (the second and third days of Eid) 130
The first departure (*al-nafr al-awwal*) 132
The third day of *al-Tashrīq* (the fourth day of Eid) 134
The second departure (*al-nafr al-thānī*) 134
The umrah of someone performing hajj only (*mufrid*) 135
The Farewell *Ṭawāf* (*Ṭawāf al-Wadāʿ*) 135

5: Visiting the Prophet ﷺ 139
The manner of visiting him ﷺ 140
An important point for the visitor regarding the etiquette of of his visit 145
The Sacred Precinct (*Ḥaram*) of Medina and the etiquette of staying therein 146
Visiting the historical sites 146
Bidding farewell to Medina 149
Concluding remarks 152

Glossary of Arabic Terms and Places 154

Transliteration Table

ء	’ (A distinctive glottal stop made at the bottom of the throat.)
ا	*a*, *ā*
ب	*b*
ت	*t*
ث	*th* (Pronounced like the *th* in *think*.)
ج	*j*
ح	*ḥ* (Hard *h* sound made at the Adam’s apple in the middle of the throat.)
خ	*kh* (Pronounced like the *ch* in Scottish *loch*.)
د	*d*
ذ	*dh* (Pronounced like the *th* in *this*.)
ر	*r*
ز	*z*
س	*s*
ش	*sh*
ص	*ṣ* (An emphatic *s* pronounced behind the upper front teeth.)
ض	*ḍ* (An emphatic *d*-like sound made by pressing the entire tongue against the upper palate.)
ط	*ṭ* (An emphatic *t* pronounced behind the front teeth.)
ظ	*ẓ* (An emphatic *th*, like the *th* in *this*, made behind the front teeth.)
ع	‘ (A distinctive Semitic sound made in the middle of the throat, sounding to a Western ear more like a vowel than a consonant.)
غ	*gh* (A guttural sound made at the top of the throat, resembling the untrilled German and French *r*.)
ف	*f*
ق	*q* (A guttural *k* sound produced at the back of the palate.)
ك	*k*
ل	*l*
م	*m*
ن	*n*
ه	*h*
و	*w*, *u*, *ū*
ي	*y*, *i*, *ī*

Translator's Introduction

In the name of Allah the All-Merciful, the Compassionate

All praise belongs to Allah, the Lord of the Worlds, and may the best blessings and perfect greetings be upon our master Muhammad, his Companions and those who follow their way with excellence.

It has been related by Abū Hurayrah ﵁ that the Messenger of Allah ﷺ said, 'Whoever performs hajj for Allah's sake and does not speak obscenely, nor commits acts of impiety (*fisq*), he returns [home] like the day his mother gave birth to him.' (An agreed upon narration.)

Moreover, Lady 'Ā'ishah ﵂ relates, 'I said, "O Messenger of Allah, we regard fighting (*jihād*) [in the way of Allah] as being the best of deeds; should we not fight [for the sake of Allah]?" He replied, "But the best struggle is an accepted hajj."' (Narrated by al-Bukhārī and al-Nasā'ī.)

The current work is the only authoritative guide readily available today to pilgrims wishing to perform hajj and umrah according to the four schools of Islamic jurisprudence, authored by Shaykh Nūr al-Dīn 'Itr, a scholar par-excellence and a polymath, considered by many as the foremost authority on Qur'anic and Hadith sciences in the Islamic world today. Although the author is primarily a Ḥanafī jurist, he is well versed in each of the other three schools of Sunni law as attested to by his more extensive work on hajj and umrah, of which this is an abridgement. In the original work, the author examines the legal justifications from the Qur'an and Sunnah purported by each school for their positions, whereas in this abridgement he restricts himself to simply mentioning their positions without delving further into their proofs and evidences.

In an attempt to broadan its benefit, by making it more conducive to the layman, who is unacquainted with the various schools of thought and would prefer to adhere to one school, the translator has altered the format of the original text: only the rulings according to the Ḥanafī school (being the predominantly adhered to school of thought, particularly in the West) have been retained in the main text. As for the positions of the other three schools of thought, Shāfiʿī, Mālikī and Ḥanbalī, they have instead been mentioned as footnotes so as not to obviate the original intent of the author. The importance of knowing the positions of these four schools of thought cannot be underestimated, particularly with regard to hajj, as mentioned by the author in his original work:

> Furthermore, the difference of opinion between the jurists reveals to us a tremendous divine wisdom, since it entails additional facilitation and ease (*rifq*) in which people are in a clear and apparent need, especially in this pillar: the pillar of hajj; because it is rare for a pilgrim to easily observe all of its rituals according to a single school of thought, which may subject people

> to inconvenience and hardship. This problem can be easily treated if we were to be flexible enough to adopt from all of the relied upon schools of law.[1]

For reasons of practicality, a supplementary booklet has been included with this translation, containing all the supplications mentioned throughout the work for the various rituals: when travelling, during *ṭawāf*, in ʿArafah and so forth, which the pilgrim may carry with him when performing them. In order to aid readers, this booklet contains the supplications in the original Arabic, as well as their English translation and transliteration.

Additional footnotes have been included by the translator, especially on the most common violations (*jināyāt*) that pilgrims may encounter during hajj and their respective penalties and expiations, which have been mainly extracted from the author's more extensive work on the subject *al-Ḥajj wa al-ʿumrah fi al-fiqh al-Islāmī* [Hajj and umrah in Islamic law]. In order to differentiate between the words of the author that were part of the original text but have now been placed as footnotes, and the translator's footnotes, I have begun the latter with '[T]' for 'Translator'. Furthermore, a glossary of Arabic terms and place names has also been appended to the work.

The reader is advised to adhere to one of the four schools of thought unless there is genuine need or hardship, which as the author said is common during hajj, in which case one may adopt the position of one of the other schools.

---

1 ʿItr, Nūr al-Dīn. *al-Ḥajj wa al-ʿumrah fi al-fiqh al-Islāmī.* 5th edn. Damascus: Dār al-Yamāmah, 1995/1416, 7–8.

Moreover, it must be said that no guide book, however authoritative it may be, dispenses with the need of studying, even if briefly, with living scholars and consulting them on ambiguous matters. This work will also serve those imams and hajj guides who may be unfamiliar with the positions of all the four schools.

Lastly, I would like to thank all those who assisted me in this work, with special thanks to: Muhammad Ridwaan, for his useful suggestions and observations on style; Andrew Booso, for copy-editing the work; Mohammed Absher Mostafa, for providing the Arabic for the supplications; Uthman Ali, for providing the transliteration for the supplications; Shaykh Maḥmūd Miṣrī, for providing the biography of the author; Mohammad Almass, for designing the cover and providing the diagrams; Naiem Qaddoura, for typesetting the current work; and Idris Kamal, for typesetting the sister booklet *The Pilgrim's Companion.*

Shaykh Nūr al-Dīn ʿItr

Born in Aleppo 1937, he obtained a bachelor's degree from the faculty of Shariah at the University of al-Azhar, where he was also awarded, with distinction, an international certificate at the level of professorship from the Department of Qur'anic Exegesis and Hadith.

He has since held many prestigious posts, including: Head of the Department of Qur'anic Exegesis and Hadith in the faculty of Shariah, University of Damascus; Head and Professor of the Department of Qur'anic Exegesis and Hadith, University Wing at the Institute of Shariah Learning, Aleppo, and the Fatḥ Islamic Institute, Damascus; Head of the faculty of Qur'anic Exegesis and its Sciences for Higher Education, and Head of the Department of Hadith for Advanced Studies, at Abū Nūr Academy, Damascus. He has and continues to supervise MA and Ph.D. students in Syria and other Arab states.

Shaykh ʿItr won both the first and the second prizes at competitions in hadith studies that were organised by the Arab organisation for culture, education and science, and has participated in many national, Arab and international seminars and conferences. He has lectured at the faculties of Shariah and fundamentals of religion at the following universities: Umm al-Qurā, Muḥammad ibn Saʿūd, Imam

Awzāʿī [in Lebanon], Kuwait, Dubai, Algeria and Marmarah University in Istanbul and many universities in India.

He is lead editor for many scholarly journals in Saudi Arabia, Kuwait, Dubai, Lebanon, Syria, Jordan and Gaza, has published many articles of his own, and is the longstanding editor for the *Islamic Encyclopaedia*, Kuwait.

He has authored over fifty scholarly works and critical editions of classical works, including: *Minhāj al-naqd fī ʿulūm al-ḥadīth* [The methodology of criticism in hadith sciences], *Imām al-Tirmidhī wa muwāzanah bayna Jāmiʿhi wa Ṣaḥīḥayn* [Imam al-Tirmidhī and the comparison between his *Compendium* and the *Ṣaḥīḥayn*], *Muʿjam al-muṣṭalaḥāt al-ḥadīthiyyah* [The dictionary of hadith terms], *ʿUlūm al-Qur'ān al-Karīm* [The sciences of the noble Qur'an], *Usūl al-jarḥ wa al-taʿdīl* [The principles of criticism and endorsement (of hadith narrators), *al-Ḥajj wa al-ʿumrah fī al-fiqh al-Islāmī* [Hajj and umrah in Islamic shariah], *ʿUlūm al-ḥadīth* [The sciences of hadith, by Ibn al-Ṣalāḥ], *al-Riḥlah li ṭalab al-ḥadīth* [Journeying in search of hadith, by al-Baghdādī], *Sharḥ ʿilal al-Tirmidhī* [The commentary on subtle discrepancies, by Ibn Rajab al-Ḥanbalī], *Nuzhah al-naẓar fī tawḍīḥ nukhbah al-fikr* [The pleasure of the gaze in exposition of the select thoughts, by Ibn Ḥajar], *Irshād ṭullāb al-ḥaqā'iq* [Guiding the seekers of truths, by al-Nawawī], *Manāhij al-muḥaddithīn* [The methodologies of the hadith specialists], *Mādha ʿan al-mar'ah* [What about women?], *Fikr al-muslim wa taḥiddiyāt al-alf al-thālithah* [Muslim thought and the challenges of the third millennium] and his acclaimed magnum opus *Iʿlām al-anām* [Announcement to mankind] a commentary upon Ḥāfiẓ Ibn Ḥajr's *Bulūgh al-marām* [Attainment of the goal].

Author's Introduction

In the name of Allah, the All-Merciful, the Compassionate

All praise belongs to Allah, who enables the one who has accepted His invitation for hajj and umrah to His house. May Allah send His blessings and salutations upon our master Muhammad, the one sent as a caller to Allah's guidance and mercy, his family and Companions, and those who adhere to his Sacred Law and follow the path of his Sunnah.

To proceed: Allah, the Transcendent and Exalted, does not accept any deed that is performed contrary to the Sacred Law, regardless of how frequently or strenuously one performs such an act or spends one's wealth in that regard. This ultimate purpose of the slave is only achieved by knowing the rulings of the Sacred Law: in that which he performs and that from which he abstains. So what about [about knowing the rulings of] hajj, the opportunity of a lifetime and the expiator for all sins of the past! The scholars of all schools of law have categorically stated that it is necessary for a pilgrim to know the rulings of hajj.

I have repeatedly been asked to author a concise book that would be easy for a pilgrim to carry and read whilst stationary and travelling, during his *ṭawāf*, *saʿy*[2] and the rest of his rites. Since I saw a pressing need for such a work, I have accordingly responded to the tremendous objective and have presented for the pilgrim this detailed and systemic [guide], beginning with one's departure as a traveller, to returning safely to one's family. I have presented herein the rites of hajj according to a daily schedule, explaining the rituals that one needs to observe on each of the days, so as to make matters clearer and easier to apply, without delving into derived rulings and particular case scenarios. We have included important amendments and instructions in this edition[3] that will help one avoid encountering difficulties.

Dear reader, if you desire to study the rulings in greater detail, then you may refer to my more comprehensive work entitled *al-Ḥajj wa al-ʿumrah fī al-fiqh al-Islāmī* [Hajj and umrah in Islamic jurisprudence], which has been printed repeatedly and has been acclaimed and endorsed by the scholars, for which all praise is due to Allah.

I ask Allah the Unblemished, the Exalted, the Generous, the Beneficent, to spread far and wide its benefit and that of the original [more comprehensive work], and that He graciously accepts it and rewards this attempt to serve this great pillar [of Islam]. Indeed, He is the Most Generous of the Generous and the Most Merciful of the Merciful.

Servant of the Qur'an and Hadith Nūr al-Dīn ʿItr
Faculty of Shariah, University of Damascus

---

2 [T] The going between the two hills al-Ṣafā and al-Marwah, which are situated adjacent to the Kaaba. Today pilgrims will find that there is a concourse that has been built and connects the two to facilitate ease in performing the *saʿy*.

3 [T] Namely, the third edition, printed in Damascus in 1996.

1

The Fundamental Rulings of Hajj

The obligation to perform hajj and its pre-requisites

Hajj is the fifth pillar of Islam. It is unique in that it is an act of worship that requires the use of one's body and wealth, as one undertakes the journey, performs the rites and endures the struggle.

Hajj, according to the Sacred Law, is to intend [the journey to] 'the Ancient House' (*al-Bayt al-'Atīq*)[4] to perform the obligatory acts, such as standing in 'Arafah[5] and circumambulating the Kaaba (*ṭawāf*), all the while in a state of *iḥrām*[6] and with the intention to perform hajj.

It is a categorical and definitive obligation; Allah Most High has said: *Mankind owes [it to] Allah to perform pilgrimage (hajj) to the House, for whoever is able to find a*

---

4 [T] The Ancient House is synonymous with the Kaaba and is amongst the many epithets used to describe 'the House of Allah' in the Qur'an, which include: Kaaba (the Cube), *al-Bayt* (the House), *al-Bayt al-Ḥarām* (the Sacred House), *al-Bayt al-Ma'mūr* (the Oft-Visited House), and *al-Bayt al-'Atīq* (the Ancient House).

5 [T] The name of a plain, approximately thirteen miles southeast of Mecca.

6 [T] *Iḥrām* is a condition for both hajj and umrah to be valid. For definition of *iḥrām* (see p. 8).

way (Qur'an 3:97). It is a religious obligation upon a 'legally responsible'[7] Muslim to perform it once in a lifetime, and that is by way of Allah facilitating matters for this nation and honouring it.

The virtue of hajj is immense, and the hadiths regarding that are profuse. We shall mention some of them below.

It has been related by Abū Hurayrah ﵁ that the Messenger of Allah ﷺ said, 'Whoever performs hajj for Allah's sake and does not speak obscenely, nor commits [acts of] impiety (*fisq*), he returns [home] like the day his mother gave birth to him.' (An agreed upon narration.)[8] And it has been related on the authority of ʿAbd-Allāh ibn Masʿūd ﵁ that the Prophet ﷺ said, 'Follow up hajj with umrah, as they eradicate poverty and sins just as a bellow (*kīr*) eradicates impurities from steel, gold and silver. There is no reward for an accepted hajj except Paradise.' (Narrated by al-Nasāʾī and Ibn Mājah, as well as Ibn Khuzaymah and Ibn Ḥibbān in their respective *Ṣaḥīḥ* collections.)

Hastening to perform hajj

Hajj is incumbent as soon as possible upon whoever meets the conditions for its obligation.[9] Thus, if one delays it till the following year, one is sinful and disobedient.

---

7 [T] A person who is sane and pubescent.

8 [T] *Muttafaq ʿalayhi* is a technical hadith term used to describe a hadith that is narrated by both Imams al-Bukhārī and Muslim in their respective *Ṣaḥīḥ* hadith collections; such hadiths are considered to be the highest category of rigorously authenticated (*ṣaḥīḥ*).

9 The Mālikīs and Ḥanbalīs agree with the Ḥanafīs on this. The Shāfiʿīs, however, are of the opinion that it is not obligatory to perform it as soon as possible, and one is not sinful for postponing it till the following year. Laymen are mistaken in their assumption that al-Shāfiʿī

The conditions for the obligation to perform hajj

The conditions for the obligation to perform hajj (and similarly umrah according to those who consider it to be necessary) are five:

1. sanity;
2. Islam: these first two are conditions for its obligation and likewise its validity; hence, hajj is not valid from a disbeliever or an insane person;
3. having reached puberty;
4. freedom: hence, hajj is not obligatory upon a child or a slave, though if they were to perform it, it will be valid as a voluntary (*nafl*) pilgrimage. Therefore, it is necessary for them to perform the obligatory pilgrimage after puberty and emancipation, respectively. This applies to a child who has reached the age of discrimination.[10] As for a child who hasn't reached the age of discrimination, then his guardian enters *iḥrām* on his behalf, though subject to details which we have left out here;
5. and ability, which can be summarised as possession of provisions and transport. It is only conditional for its [hajj] obligation; however, the lifting of its obligation

---

allows hajj to be postponed unconditionally; on the contrary, the Shāfiʿīs only allow one to postpone hajj on the condition that one has the determination and resolve to perform it in the future, and not that one disregards or is indifferent to performing it (as is the case with many people) and on the condition that one does not fear inability [in performing it in future] or lack of wealth. Therefore, if any of these conditions are unfulfilled, it will be unlawful for one to postpone it, which makes it necessary for a Muslim to take caution against postponing hajj beyond the time when one is immediately able to perform it.

10 [T] Approximately seven years of age.

is not dependent on it; thus, if someone for whom the conditions of ability are not met performs hajj, then his hajj will be valid, and he will be absolved of its obligation.

There are two additional conditions for the obligation to perform hajj that apply solely to women, and these are from amongst the characteristics classified under 'ability' that do not apply to men. They are:

1. for her to be accompanied by her husband[11] or an unmarriageable male relative (*maḥram*)[12] if the distance of the journey is eighty-one kilometres or more;

---

11 The Shāfiʿīs are flexible regarding the condition of a member of unmarriageable-kin accompanying a lady, for they have said: If she finds trustworthy women (two or more) with whom she feels secure, then that would suffice with regard to the obligation to perform the hajj of Islam [the obligatory hajj]. This is similar to the position of the Mālikīs. However, we find strength in the Ḥanafī and Ḥanbalī positions, especially considering what is known of congestion, risks and other dangers. Nevertheless, it is necessary to pay attention to the fact that this flexibility is particular to the obligatory hajj; as for a voluntary hajj, then it is not lawful for a woman to travel for it without her husband or an unmarriageable male relative according to the agreement of all schools of thought; she would be sinful if she was to contravene that, and her hajj would not be accepted (*mabrūr*).

12 [T] Those considered both legally invalid and permanently unlawful for a woman to marry are: (1) father, grandfather and upwards, (2) son, grandson and downwards, (3) brother, (4) paternal uncle, or brother of any male ancestor, (5) maternal uncle or any brother of a female ancestor, (6) paternal and maternal nephews or any other descendants of brothers or sisters, (7) step-father, husband to grandmother etc. (8) son in-law or husband to other female descendant, (9) husband's father, grandfather, etc. (10) stepsons and descendants, (11) any unmarriageable kin to her through breastfeeding during infancy or her having acted as a wet-nurse to him.

2. for her not to be in her post-divorce or mourning [her husband's death] waiting period.[13] Hence, if the conditions for the obligation to perform hajj are not met except when she is in her waiting period, or her waiting period is at a time when it is possible for her travel for hajj, then it is not obligatory upon her to perform it.

We also want to highlight certain matters that are conditional for hajj to be obligatory for one to perform in person, and these are:

1. good health;
2. safety en-route;
3. not [physically] prevented by the ruler or from fear of him;
4. [accompanied by] a trustworthy unmarriageable male relative or husband, in the case of a woman;
5. (also in the case of a woman) that she is not in her waiting period [after divorce or husband's death].

If any of these conditions are unfulfilled, it would not be necessary for one to perform hajj in person; rather, one would be obliged to either send someone else to perform it on one's behalf or leave a bequest for it to be performed on one's behalf after death.

---

13 A period in which a woman waits before being allowed to re-marry. In the case of a divorcée, the waiting period is three menstrual cycles, childbirth if pregnant or three months if after menopause; as for a bereaving widow, it is four months and ten days or childbirth if pregnant.

The conditions for the validity of hajj

The following are conditional for the validity of hajj:

1. Islam;
2. sanity, and these two have already been explained;
3. and *iḥrām,* which is the most well-known of these conditions and often misunderstood by people: some think that it is merely wearing the special garb for *iḥrām* [which is not the case].

Iḥrām is, in reality, in relation to hajj or umrah similar to what the intention is for the prayer: it is the intention[14] accompanied by the *talbiyah*;[15] and it is absolutely necessary that the *talbiyah* accompany the intention for one to commence this act of worship.

In order to enter into *iḥrām* one must intend to perform hajj in one's heart, while simultaneously reciting,

اَللَّهُمَّ إِنِّيْ أُرِيْدُ الْحَجَّ فَيَسِّرْهُ لِيْ وَتَقَبَّلْهُ مِنِّيْ إِنَّكَ أَنْتَ السَّمِيْعُ الْعَلِيْمُ.
لَبَّيْكَ اللَّهُمَّ لَبَّيْكَ، لَبَّيْكَ لَا شَرِيْكَ لَكَ لَبَّيْكَ، إِنَّ الْحَمْدَ
وَالنِّعْمَةَ لَكَ وَالْـمُلْكَ، لَا شَرِيْكَ لَكَ.

O Allah, I intend to perform hajj, so facilitate it for me and accept it from me. Indeed, You are the All-Hearing, the All-Knowing. Ever at Your service, O Allah, ever at

---

14 As for the Shāfiʿīs and Ḥanbalīs, the *iḥrām* is merely the intention and does not depend on the *talbiyah*; rather, the *talbiyah* is one of the sunnahs of *iḥrām* according to them. According to the Mālikīs, the *talbiyah* is necessary in and of itself, while it is sunnah that it accompany the *iḥrām*.

15 [T] To recite the formula '*Labbayka Allāhumma labbayk...*', 'Ever at Your service, O Allah, ever at Your service...'

Your service. Ever at your service, You have no partner,
ever at Your service. Indeed, all praise and blessings
belong to You, and [likewise] the dominion.
You have no partner.

The appointed time for *iḥrām* is the time when the hajj rites are performed, which Allah Most High has explained in His words: *The pilgrimage is [in] the well-known months* (Qur'an 2:197). These are Shawwāl, Dhū al-Qaʿdah and the first ten days of Dhū al-Ḥijjah according to the vast majority of the Companions, their Followers and the subsequent generations.

As for the designated sites for *iḥrām*, namely those places which a person intending hajj or umrah is not allowed to pass except in *iḥrām*, then each group of pilgrims coming from a particular geographical location has its own designated site from which it must enter *iḥrām*; and they are as follows:

a. the designated *iḥrām* site for the people of Medina is Dhū al-Ḥulayfah, which is now known as ʿĀbār ʿAlī (the Wells of ʿAlī). It is seven kilometres from Medina and approximately four hundred and forty kilometres from Mecca;
b. the designated *iḥrām* site for the people of Greater Syria (Shām) is al-Juḥfah: it is situated close to the seashore, halfway between Mecca and Medina. Al-Juḥfah has been effaced, so the pilgrims from the lands of Shām, the Turks, and the people of Egypt and Morocco enter *iḥrām* from a town called Rābigh, which is a little before al-Juḥfah. It is two hundred and twenty kilometres from Mecca;

c. the designated *iḥrām* site for the people of Iraq is Dhāt ʿIrq, which is a distance of ninety-four kilometres from Mecca;
d. the designated *iḥrām* site for the people of Najd is Qarn al-Manāzil,[16] which is ninety-four kilometres from Mecca;
e. and the designated *iḥrām* site for the people of Yemen is Yalamlam, which is ninety-four kilometres from Mecca.

Whoever passes by one of these sites, intending hajj or umrah and is not from amongst its residents, enters *iḥrām* from that site by which he passes. So if a Syrian enters from the route of Yalamlam, for instance, he enters *iḥrām* from it.

Whoever passes a designated *iḥrām* site without *iḥrām*, and does not return to it to enter *iḥrām* from it, is sinful and obliged to offer a sacrifice by consensus.[17]

Whoever is within the regions between the designated *iḥrām* sites and Mecca is to enter *iḥrām* from home. If, however, someone in Mecca wants to perform umrah, he is obliged to leave the region of *al-Ḥaram*[18] to the nearest place inside *al-Ḥill*[19] and then enter *iḥrām* for umrah *from there.*

---

16 [T] A region east of Medina; the capital of Saudi Arabia, Riyadh, is located within Najd itself.

17 [T] The sacrificing of an animal is required for breaching certain rules and regulations of hajj so as to redress those shortcomings; a detailed discussion will follow.

18 [T] The Sacred Precinct is an area with defined borders (see Figure 1 and 2).

19 [T] The area between the Sacred Precinct and the various *mīqāts* [*iḥrām* sites].

Entering *iḥrām* before the designated *iḥrām* sites is valid by consensus. The Ḥanafīs have said that this early entry into *iḥrām* is better if one is confident in not violating the rules and regulations demanded by being in the state of *iḥrām*.[20]

The obligation to enter *iḥrām* from a designated *iḥrām* site is agreed upon [amongst the scholars] in relation to someone who intends to visit Mecca for the [hajj or umrah] rites.

As for someone who intends to come to Mecca or the area of 'the Sacred Precinct' (*al-Ḥaram*) surrounding it for some need other than hajj or umrah, the Ḥanafīs opine that it is necessary to enter *iḥrām* for umrah,[21] if he does not do so for hajj. The Ḥanafīs have, nevertheless, exempted someone who is within the region of the *iḥrām* sites, as it is permissible for him, according to them, to enter Mecca without *iḥrām* for his particular need. Accordingly, if a pilgrim was to travel from Mecca to Jeddah to buy, or sell, or reserve a flight or the like and then return to Mecca, intending to extend his previous stay therein, it would not be necessary to re-enter *iḥrām* for umrah according to them, since he has come to Mecca from within the region of the *iḥrām* sites.[22]

---

20 The other three Imams are of the opinion that it is better for one not to enter *iḥrām* before the designated *iḥrām* site.

21 The Mālikīs and Ḥanbalīs are in agreement with the Ḥanafīs.

22 The Shāfiʿīs are of the opinion that if one intends to come to Mecca or the region of the Sacred Precinct for some need other than hajj or umrah, then it is not necessary for him to initiate *iḥrām* to enter it.

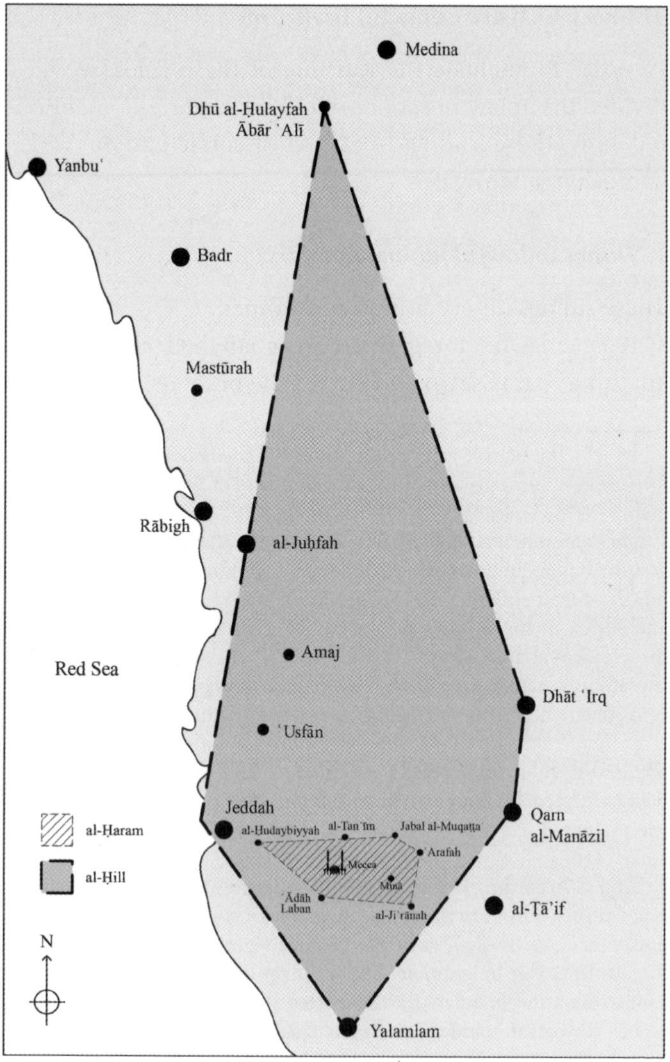

Figure 1: The designated sites (*al-Mawāqīt*) from where pilgrims need to enter into *iḥrām*

Things which are unlawful in *iḥrām*

In order to facilitate the learning of these rules, we have divided the unlawful actions into five categories,[23] mentioning only those rulings that are essential and in which confusion often arises.

1. *Things unlawful for one to wear*

These rulings differ for men and women.[24]

It is unlawful for men to wear stitched clothing and anything that is sewn and covers the body or a limb, such

---

23 [T] The Islamic jurists have stipulated the necessity of atonement for whoever commits any of the unlawful acts of *iḥrām*, as long as it is before the 'two releases' (see p. 129), or neglects any of the necessary acts in hajj or umrah. If contraventions are committed intentionally, then one is sinful and required to expiate and repent. Willingness to discharge the *fidyah* [atonement] does not absolve one of being considered disobedient and sinful. Imam al-Nawawī says, 'Some layman may commit some of these unlawful acts and say, "I will expiate," under the illusion that by expiating he will escape from the consequence of committing an act of disobedience. This is a blatant error and abhorrent ignorance. The atonement does not allow one to commit an unlawful action…, and whoever does anything ruled to be unlawful has precluded his hajj from being accepted.' al-Nawawī. *Mukhtasar īḍāḥ*, 58. ʿItr, Nūr al-Dīn. *al-Ḥajj wa al-ʿumrah fī al-fiqh al-Islāmī*. 5th edn. Damascus: Dār al-Yamāmah, 1995/1416, 134.

24 [T] According to the Ḥanafīs, if a pilgrim wears any of the clothes unlawful for him in *iḥrām* for a whole day or night [or the duration of one of them, such as half a day plus half of a night], whether intentionally, forgetfully or due to ignorance of the ruling, then it is necessary for him to sacrifice a sheep; unless it was due to a medical reason, in which case he has the option to offer a sacrifice, fast three days or distribute three *ṣāʿ*s of wheat [one *ṣāʿ* is equivalent to four kilograms] to six poor people [or its value in money]. Similarly is the case of a woman who wears a face veil that touches her skin; however, if they wear it for less than a full day or night, then the Ḥanafīs stipulate that giving away *ṣadaqah* is sufficient.

as socks, head covering, face covering and wearing shoes that reach up to the two *ka ʿbs* (which has been interpreted by the Ḥanafis as the protruding bone at the centre of the upper part of the foot).

As for a woman, it is only unlawful for her to wear a face veil that touches her skin.[25] However, if a woman wears a face veil that does not touch her skin, then it is not unlawful. This is similar to what many women practise, as they place on their forehead a wide cap with a veil draping over it, such that it covers the face without touching it.

It is not offensive for a woman in *iḥrām* to wear gold and silver and adorn herself with jewellery according to the majority of scholars, though it is unlawful for her to display her beautification in *iḥrām* before non-relatives and marriageable kin; otherwise, her hajj will not be accepted (*mabrūr*).[26]

According to the schools of al-Shāfiʿī and Aḥmad, an atonement (*fidyah*) is necessary, which according to them and the Mālikīs is either a sacrifice, fasting three days or distributing three *ṣāʿ*s of wheat to six poor people for merely wearing it, even for a moment. The Mālikīs have only obligated this *fidyah* if one benefits from wearing the clothing in warding off heat or cold, as opposed to (for example) wearing a very fine shirt; otherwise, an atonement is unnecessary, unless he wears it for a full day. ʿItr, Nūr al-Dīn. *al-Ḥajj wa al-ʿumrah fī al-fiqh al-Islāmī*, 139. A day, according to Islamic law, is from sunrise to sunset, and a night is from sunset to dawn. Burhānī, Muḥammad Hishām. *al-Ḥajj, al-ziyārah wa al-ʿumrah*. 5th edn. Damascus: n.p. 1997/1419, 129.

25 And similarly the wearing of gloves according to the other three schools.

26 [T] Meaning, unaccepted in terms of her being rewarded and not that its legal fulfilment and her being discharged from her obligation are unaccepted.

AN IMPORTANT CLARIFICATION FOR MEN REGARDING THE RULING OF TYING THE UPPER AND LOWER GARMENT

It is offensive for someone in the state of *iḥrām* to tie the two ends of his lower garment, to tie a belt around it or to fasten it with pins or buttons, though nothing [in terms of expiation] is required of him if he was to do so, and similarly is the case with the upper garment. As for inserting the two ends of the upper garment into the lower garment, then it is permissible.[27]

The prohibition in wearing a turban applies to any head covering. As for shading one's head with something that does not touch it, such as an umbrella, then it entails no offence.

---

27 The Shāfiʿīs and Ḥanbalīs differentiate between the lower and upper garment: the Shāfiʿīs allow someone in a state of *iḥrām* to tie the lower garment and fasten around it a string so that it stays up, or that one makes for it [something] similar to a *ḥujzah* (continuous-belt loop) and inserts in it a waistband for stability, or closes it with a button or spaced out buttons, or inserts one end of his upper garment into his lower garment. It is not permissible for him to hold up the lower garment with a pin, a needle or a safety pin. Neither is it lawful to tie the upper garment or pierce it with a pin, needle or a safety pin, or to tie one end of it to another with a string or something else. If he does anything of the above-mentioned things that are unlawful for him, it would become necessary for him to expiate. The Ḥanbalīs have said that he is allowed to tie his lower garment, as he needs it to cover his nakedness, and likewise to fasten its centre with a rope without tying it; however, he may insert some of it into the other, though it is not permissible for him to tie, button or pierce his upper garment, whether with a pin or something else, such as a needle or safety pin; and he shouldn't insert its two ends into his lower garment. The Mālikīs state that an expiation is necessary with regard to all of the above, whether it was in the lower garment or the upper garment.

Similar to wearing the turban is covering the face.[28]

The prohibition in wearing saffron also applies to clothing that is perfumed; hence, it is impermissible to wear it.

If wearing a pair of *khuffs* is impermissible,[29] then the prohibition in wearing gloves is even more emphatic, because there is a greater need for *khuffs*; as opposed to wearing gloves, which are an obvious extravagance. Cutting the *khuffs* below the two *kaʿbs* has been interpreted by the Ḥanafis as the protruding bone at the centre of the upper part of the foot.[30]

2. *Unlawful matters pertaining to the body of someone in* **iḥrām**

It includes anything that involves perfuming the body, eliminating dishevelment and removing dirt. Consequently, the following things are unlawful:

a. shaving one's head and removing hair from any part of the body;[31]

---

28 This is according to the three Imams; the Shāfiʿīs, however, do not deem it unlawful for one in *iḥrām*.

29 [T] A pair of waterproof socks, usually made of leather, which one may wear for convenience, as it is permissible to merely wipe over them during ablution instead of washing the feet if the conditions for their validity are fulfilled.

30 Others have interpreted it as the ankles which are the end point for washing during ablution.

31 [T] According to the Ḥanafīs, it is necessary for whoever shaves a quarter of his head or beard to expiate as outlined in footnote 36 if one had a valid excuse; otherwise, it is necessary to sacrifice a sheep. It is necessary for the barber to give away *ṣadaqah* if he was in *iḥrām*; and likewise if he shaves the head of someone who is not in *iḥrām*. If one shaves [or cuts] hair that is less than a quarter of the head, it is necessary

b. removing one's nails by clipping them or applying some other method, which is akin to removing hair, because of the common factor of extravagance in both;[32]
c. and applying oil to one's hair,[33] whether on one's head or any other part of the body [such as the beard], even with something non-perfumed such as olive oil,[34] because it entails adornment and grooming the hair. Therefore, the one in the state of *iḥrām* should take extreme caution to ensure that no ghee, grease or oil is transferred to them by his hand or something else or whilst eating.

---

to give away *ṣadaqah*. However, if three hairs fall from one's head or beard when performing ablution or scratching [the head], one needs to give away a handful of wheat [or its value] for each hair. If it falls more than once on numerous occasions, one needs to give the required expiation for each occasion. If one shaves all of one's nape and armpits, or one of them, it is necessary to sacrifice a sheep, though if one shaves one of them partially, even if it is a lot, then *ṣadaqah* is necessary. According to the Mālikīs, no expiation is necessary if hair falls during ablution or when having a bath. If any hair falls without one causing it to do so, expiation is not necessary by the consensus of the schools. 'Itr, Nūr al-Dīn. *al-Ḥajj wa al-ʿumrah fī al-fiqh al-Islāmī,* 141–42.

32 [T] The Ḥanafīs have opined that if one clips all of one's nails and toenails on a single occasion, it is necessary for him to sacrifice a sheep, and likewise, if he clips all the nails of either a hand or foot. If, however, he clips less than five nails from one hand or five nails from more than a single hand or foot, it is necessary for him to give away *ṣadaqah* for each nail. 'Itr, Nūr al-Dīn. *al-Ḥajj wa al-ʿumrah fī al-fiqh al-Islāmī,* 142.

33 The Mālikīs agree with the Ḥanafīs [in this prohibition]. As for the Shāfiʿīs, they deem it lawful to apply non-perfumed oil to bodily hair with the exception of the head and beard, as it as unlawful to apply non-perfumed oil to the head and beard, even if shaved.

34 [T] If one applies non-perfumed oil to any part of the body for other than a medical reason, its ruling is that of applying perfume (according to Abū Hanīfah and Mālik). If, however, one applies it for a medicinal reason, such as applying it on a wound or cracks in the feet, an expiation is not necessary. Al-Shāfiʿī and Aḥmad (according

Applying perfume

It is unlawful for one in *iḥrām* to apply perfume on his clothing or body,[35] even for a medicinal purpose.[36] Thus,

---

to one narration) have opined that if one applies it to one's hair or beard, an expiation is necessary; if it was applied elsewhere, then it is permissible. The relied-upon opinion according to the Ḥanbalīs is the permissibility of applying non-perfumed oil to any part of the body without it necessitating an expiation. One should take note here that this difference of opinion is only with regard to non-perfumed oil; as for perfumed oils, creams, mousse and lotions, then an expiation is necessary by the agreement of the scholars, in accordance with what they have said regarding the application of perfume. ʿItr, Nūr al-Dīn. *al-Ḥajj wa al-ʿumrah fī al-fiqh al-Islāmī*, 140-41.

35 [T] The Ḥanafīs have differentiated between the application of perfume on one's body and one's clothing; as for the body, they have said that the sacrifice of a sheep is necessary if someone in *iḥrām* applies perfume on a complete limb, such as the head, leg or arm, or any part of the body that reaches the surface-area of a limb. The body is considered a [single] limb if perfumed on a single occasion (*majlis*).Otherwise, an expiation is necessary for each occasion, and it is necessary to remove the perfume before the sacrifice; otherwise, another expiation is necessary. If one applies perfume to less than a full limb, it is only necessary to give away *ṣadaqah* to the poor, due to the limited nature of the violation. The expiation becomes necessary by mere application of perfume, even if washed off immediately. As for applying perfume to one's clothing, then two conditions need to be met for it to be necessary to sacrifice: that it is a large amount, such that it covers the area of a hand span, and that it remains for a whole day or night. If any of these two conditions is not met, giving *ṣadaqah* is necessary; if neither is met, it is necessary to give away a handful of wheat [or its value] as *ṣadaqah*. The Mālikīs, Shāfiʿīs and Ḥanbalīs have unconditionally obligated atonement and have not restricted the application of perfume to a full limb or an area of hand span in clothing. ʿItr, Nūr al-Dīn. *al-Ḥajj wa al-ʿumrah fī al-fiqh al-Islāmī*, 139-140.

36 [T] In this case, one has the choice of expiating by either: sacrificing a sheep in the *Ḥaram*; giving away three *ṣāʿ*s of wheat flour

one should avoid all types of perfumed soap, including soap imported from abroad, just as it is necessary for one to take precaution when buying perfume and to refrain from sleeping on anything perfumed.

As for merely smelling perfume without touching it, then it is offensive;[37] however, it is, by consensus, permissible to smell fruits and every desert plant, such as wormwood. As for eating and drinking perfume, then it is unlawful for one in *iḥrām* by the consensus of the four schools, though if one mixes it with food before cooking it and then cooks with it, nothing is incumbent upon one [by way of expiation],[38] whether it is a small or large quantity. Similarly, if one mixes it with cooked food after cooking it. As for when one mixes it with uncooked food, then if the food is more [than the perfume], nothing is incumbent upon him, even if the fragrance is apparent, though if the fragrance is apparent, it is offensive. If, however, the perfume is more [than the food], a sacrifice is consequently necessary, even if its fragrance is not apparent.[39]

[twelve kilograms] or its value in money to six poor people; or fasting three days [the fasting and giving of charity is not restricted to the *Ḥaram* or a specific time]. Burhānī, Muḥammad Hishām. *al-Ḥajj, al-ziyārah wa al-ʿumrah*, 133.

37 This is according to the Ḥanafīs, Mālikīs and Shāfiʿīs; consequently, an expiation is not necessary according to them. Yet the Ḥanbalīs consider it unlawful to deliberately smell perfume, such as musk and camphor, and thus consider an expiation necessary.

38 This is according to the Ḥanafīs and Mālikīs.

39 The Mālikīs deem all of that unlawful and obligate an expiation. The Shāfiʿīs and the Ḥanbalīs have opined that if one mixes perfume with something else, such as food or drink and no smell or taste appears, it is not prohibited, nor is an expiation required; otherwise, it is unlawful and an expiation is necessary .

If one mixes perfume with a drink, such as rosewater or the like, it would consequently be necessary for him to expiate, whether it is a small or large amount.[40] As for eating fruits which have a pleasant smell, such as apples, quince, [bitter] orange, lemons and others, then they are permissible according to all scholars; and Allah knows best.

3. *Hunting*

Hunting is unlawful for one in *iḥrām*, whatever type of animal it may be. Furthermore, it is unlawful for him to assist anyone intending to hunt in any manner whatsoever, even by pointing [i.e. to an animal]. Similarly, it is unlawful to harm or drive away game and for someone in *iḥrām* to eat land-game hunted by someone in *iḥrām* or hunted *for him* by someone not in *iḥrām*.

However, the permissibility of killing five types of animal has been established for both someone in or out of *iḥrām*, in both *al-Ḥill* and *al-Ḥaram*, by the words of the hadith, 'Five kinds of beast, all of them are *fāsiq*[41] they are killed in *al-Ḥaram*: the crow, the kite, the scorpion, the rat, and the wild dog,' (an agreed upon tradition) and in another narration, 'the snake'. According to Abū Dāwūd, there is an addition [to the above narration] of 'a hostile animal', meaning a predatory animal, and they [the four schools] have agreed upon the permissibility of killing all of the above-mentioned.

---

40 This is according to the Ḥanafīs and Mālikīs.

41 Here meaning, they are excluded from those animals prohibited for one to kill and are therefore lawful to kill, even by someone in *iḥrām* or in *al-Ḥaram*.

It is lawful for one in *iḥrām* to slaughter domestic animals, such as livestock and chickens.

4. *Sexual intercourse and foreplay*

The following are classified under the prohibition of this category:

a. intercourse, which is unlawful for one in *iḥrām* and invalidates one's hajj by scholarly consensus,[42] and one is further obliged to:

    i. continue in its completion;
    ii. make it up [the following year or thereafter];
    iii. and sacrifice a camel.

---

42 [T] This is if he has intercourse before the standing in ʿArafah; if, however, he has intercourse after the standing in ʿArafah but before 'the first release' (see p. 129 for the definition of 'the first release'), his hajj is not invalidated according to the Ḥanafīs; rather, it is necessary for him to sacrifice a camel or a cow. The Mālikīs, Shāfiʿīs and Ḥanbalīs are of the opinion that his hajj is invalidated in this instance, and he is additionally obliged to sacrifice a camel or a cow. However, all the four schools concur that one's hajj is not invalidated if he has intercourse after 'the first release', though it is necessary for him to sacrifice a sheep according to the Ḥanafīs, Shāfiʿīs and Ḥanbalīs. As for foreplay [literally the direct preliminaries, i.e. to intercourse], such as kissing, fondling out of desire and for both sex organs to come into contact without a barrier, though without penetration, then it is necessary to sacrifice a sheep, whether he ejaculates or not, and his hajj is not invalidated according to the Ḥanafīs, Shāfiʿīs and Ḥanbalīs; the Ḥanbalīs, however, obligate the sacrifice of a camel or cow. The Mālikīs have said that if he ejaculates, his hajj is invalidated; otherwise, he is obliged to sacrifice a camel or cow. As for indirect preliminaries, such as looking or thinking out of desire, then the Ḥanafīs and Shāfiʿīs opine that atonement is not necessary, even if they lead to him ejaculating, which is also the Ḥanbalīs' position. ʿItr, Nūr al-Dīn. *al-Ḥajj wa al-ʿumrah fī al-fiqh al-Islāmī*, 149-53.

b. all types of foreplay are unlawful for one in *Iḥrām,* such as touching out of desire and kissing;
c. and lewd speech is also unlawful for one in *iḥrām* and should be avoided under all circumstances.

5. *Acts of impiety (*fisq*) and disputation*

Impiety is disobedience [to Allah], which is unlawful under all circumstances, though in *iḥrām* it is even more abhorrent.

Disputation is to argue with one's companion or any person such that one makes him angry; and likewise, argumentation and swearing, because of His Most High's words: *Do not speak obscenely, nor commit disobedience or dispute during hajj* (Qur'an 2:197).

Things which are lawful in *iḥrām*

Apart from the aforementioned unlawful things, everything [that is normally permissible] is permissible for one in *iḥrām*, and it is impermissible to prohibit anything in addition to the stipulated prohibitions in *iḥrām.*

However, there are certain matters which many people assume are unlawful for one in *iḥrām,* while in reality they are not; on the contrary, they are permissible; we shall mention some of them:

1. having a bath;
2. scratching one's head or body; however, one should do so gently so that no hairs fall and thus necessitate an expiation;[43]

43 [T] The expiation here is *ṣadaqah,* which is a date if only one hair falls, and a palm full of wheat [or its value]–for each hair– if three hairs

3. applying non-perfumed antimony (kohl) to the eyes;
4. and wearing a ring on the finger is considered permissible by them [the scholars] because it is not regarded as 'wearing', and so is the case with wearing a watch.

The integrals of hajj

The integrals of hajj are those matters upon which its validity depends and are its essential elements. No one is exempt from them, even due to an excuse, nor can one compensate for them by expiating or offering a sacrifice.

There are two integrals:[44]

1. standing in ʿArafah;[45]
2. the *Ṭawāf* of Departure (*Ṭawāf al-Ifāḍah*).[46]

---

fall; and if more than three fall, then the expiation is the equivalent of *ṣadaqah al-fiṭr,* which is two kilograms of whole wheat, or flour; or four kilograms of dates, raisins, barley or their equivalent for each hair that falls; though if the hair falls by itself, then an expiation is not necessary. The *ṣadaqah* can be given to any poor person, from anywhere and at any time.

44 The Mālikīs and the Ḥanbalīs have added to that the *iḥrām* and *saʿy,* while according to the Shāfiʿīs, they are six: the *iḥrām* for hajj, i.e. the intention to commence it, (which according to the Ḥanafīs is a condition), standing in ʿArafah, *ṭawāf, saʿy,* shaving or shortening the hair and observing order between the performance of most of the integrals.

45 [T] What is meant by *standing* here is to be present in ʿArafah and not literally to stand.

46 [T] Literally 'the pouring out', as people pour out in droves from Minā to Mecca for its performance. It is also called the *Ṭawāf* of the Visit (*Ṭawāf al-Ziyārah*).

The necessary acts (*wājibāt*) in hajj

They are those matters whose performance is required and whose omission is unlawful. Nonetheless, hajj is not invalidated by the omission of a necessary act; rather, whoever omits such an act is sinful and must offer a sacrifice to redress its omission, whether one omits deliberately, unintentionally, accidentally or forgetfully, unless one omits it due to a valid legal (*sharʿī*) reason. In the case of omission due to a valid legal reason, it is not necessary for one to expiate. Examples of valid legal reasons for omission include someone not walking during the *ṭawāf* or *saʿy* due to sickness, old age or feet having been amputated; and similarly, someone missing the standing in al-Muzdalifah [after dawn on the Day of Sacrifice] because of leaving for Minā during the night from fear of congestion or physical weakness, especially in the case of old men and women.

We will divide the necessary acts during hajj into two categories: fundamental and supplementary.

As for the fundamentally necessary acts, these are acts necessary in and of themselves; they are five:[47]

1. the walk (*saʿy)* between al-Ṣafā and al-Marwah;
2. standing in al-Muzdalifah;
3. stoning the sites (*jimār*);[48]

---

47 The Ḥanbalīs have similarly concurred with the Ḥanafīs with the exception of the *saʿy*, as it is an integral according to them, and they and the Mālikīs have also included amongst them [the necessary acts] spending the nights of *Tashrīq* in Minā.

48 [T] The *jimār* (plural of *jamrah*) are either the stones themselves, which are thrown at the sites or the sites enclosed by circular walls, wherein the pillars stand; what is not meant is the pillars, as is commonly misunderstood.

4. shaving or shortening the hair;
5. and the Farewell *Ṭawāf (Ṭawāf al-Wadāʿ).*

As for the supplementary necessary acts, then these are necessary acts that supplement the obligatory or fundamentally necessary hajj acts and relate to the manner in which the obligatory acts are to be performed. They are the following matters:

1. *Regarding the* iḥrām

a. initiating the *iḥrām* from one of the designated *iḥrām* sites [or before it];
b. and abstaining from unlawful acts during *iḥrām.*

Both of these are necessary by consensus.

2. *Regarding the* ṭawāf

a. performing it from the right side,[49] that is the one performing *ṭawāf* walks on the right of the Kaaba, turning his left side towards the direction of the Kaaba;
b. completing its seven cycles;
c. purification from both minor and major ritual impurity, menses and lochia; as for purification from physical impurities on one's clothing or body, then the majority Ḥanafī scholars are of the opinion that it is an emphasised sunnah;
d. covering one's nakedness [*ʿawrah*];[50]

---

49 I.e. anti-clockwise.

50 [T] The *ʿawrah* of a man is between the navel and the knee (and including the knee); as for a woman, her *ʿawrah* is the entire body with the exception of her face, hands and feet.

e. for the *Ḥijr*[51] to be within one's *ṭawāf* [i.e. circumambulating it].[52]
f. commencing it from the Black Stone;[53]
g. walking, for whoever is able ;[54]
h. performing the two cycles of prayer after the *ṭawāf*;[55]
i. and performing the *Ṭawāf* of the Visit (*Ṭawāf al-Ziyārah*)' (i.e. the integral [also known as the *Ṭawāf* of the Departure (*Ṭawāf al-Ifāḍah*)]) during the Days of Sacrifice[56] according to Abū Ḥanīfah.[57]

3. *Necessary acts during the standing in ʿArafah*

a. prolonging the standing in ʿArafah till sunset; this is for whoever stood there before sunset;[58]

---

51 Also called the *Ḥaṭīm*, it is the semi-circular wall around the northern side of the Kaaba.

52 All of the aforementioned matters are obligatory and conditional for the validity of the *ṭawāf* according to the other three schools of thought.

53 This is according to the Ḥanafīs and Mālikīs, while it is a condition according to the Shāfiʿīs and the Ḥanbalīs

54 This is according to the Ḥanafīs and Mālikīs, whereas the Shāfiʿīs consider it a sunnah.

55 The Mālikīs agree with the Ḥanafīs, while the Shāfiʿīs and the Ḥanbalīs regard them [the two cycles of prayer] as sunnah. The Mālikīs, additionally, consider the consecutive performance of the *ṭawāf* and the two cycles of prayer after it as necessary, which is a sunnah according to the Ḥanafīs.

56 [T] These are the tenth, eleventh and twelfth of Dhū al-Ḥijjah.

57 The Mālikīs have extended the time for its performance till the end of Dhū al-Ḥijjah. The Shāfiʿīs, Ḥanbalīs and the two students of Abū Ḥanīfah have opined that nothing is necessary [i.e. expiation] for postponing the *Ifāḍah* (the obligatory *ṭawāf*) till after the Days of Sacrifice and Dhū al-Ḥijjah, even though one remains in the state of *iḥrām* by consensus, subject to details that are inappropriate to mention here.

58 The Ḥanbalīs agree with the Ḥanafīs, whereas the Mālikīs have said that standing after sunset is obligatory and to do so before it is

b. and postponing[59] the sunset prayer till nightfall and performing them [the sunset and nightfall prayers] in al-Muzdalifah as a delayed combination; consequently, the sunset prayer is not valid except if delayed till nightfall.

4. *Necessary acts in Minā*

The acts to be performed in Minā are:

a. stoning the sites;[60]
b. offering a sacrifice (necessary for anyone performing hajj and umrah combined (*qārin*) or individually (*mutamatti*ʿ);[61]
c. and shaving one's head [or shortening one's hair].

The following acts are necessary in [Minā]:

a. stoning the site of ʿAqabah before shaving in the case of someone performing hajj only;
b. shaving [or shortening one's hair] during the Days of Sacrifice;[62]

---

necessary. The Shāfiʿīs have said that it is a sunnah for whoever stands before sunset to continue standing till sunset.

59 This position is one of the Ḥanafīs. The other three schools consider this combination to be a sunnah.

60 [T] These are in Minā, where Muslims perform the symbolic act of stoning the three sites that mark the three locations where Satan appeared to the Prophet Ibrāhīm ﷺ and his family, when he threw seven stones at Satan.

61 [T] For more details on the three different methods of performing pilgrimage, (see pp. 34-35).

62 According to the Ḥanafīs and likewise the Mālikīs, whereas the Shāfiʿīs and the Ḥanbalīs are of the opinion that it is a sunnah.

c. shaving one's head in *al-Ḥaram*, i.e. Mecca and the Sacred Precinct surrounding it;[63]
d. order between the following rituals:
   i. stoning;
   ii. offering a sacrifice if one is performing umrah and hajj similtaneously or umrah only (as for someone performing hajj only, then the sacrificial offering (*hadyī*) is not necessary for him);
   iii. and shaving one's head or shortening the hair.

If one neglects this order, it is necessary to offer a sacrifice;[64]

e. and not postponing the stoning [of the sites] on any of its days till the dawn of the following day.[65]

The sunnahs of hajj

A sunnah is an act whose performance is recommended, and for whose performance a legally responsible person is rewarded and whose deliberate omission entails offence, though no expiation is necessary for such an omission.

---

63 The Shāfiʿīs are of the opinion that it is preferable and not necessary.

64 As for the Shāfiʿīs, they have opined that this order is a sunnah.

65 According to Mālikīs, one does not postpone it till sunset of the same day. As for the Shāfiʿīs and the Ḥanbalīs, they have not prescribed any expiation as consequently necessary and have said that the stoning within the time of each day is a sunnah, and the time of stoning extends to the last day of *Tashrīq*, namely the fourth day of the Eid ul-Adha; thus if the sun on the final day of *Tashrīq* sets, it will no longer be valid to stone the sites and one would be obliged to expiate for any stoning missed.

The fundamental sunnahs of hajj

1. The *Ṭawāf of* Arrival (*Ṭawāf al-Qudūm*), which is a sunnah for a traveller coming from outside the designated *iḥrām* sites, who is in *iḥrām* for hajj, whether he is performing hajj only or hajj and umrah simultaneously.[66]

   Whoever proceeds directly to ʿArafah for the standing [i.e. without first coming to Mecca] is exempt from it [the *Ṭawāf* of Arrival].[67]

2. The imam's sermons. All of these three [sermons] are in the afternoon:

   a. in Mecca on the seventh of Dhū al-Ḥijjah, wherein he teaches [the pilgrims] the rites they need to perform;
   b. on the Day of ʿArafah in ʿArafāt: these two sermons are similar to the Friday sermon;
   c. and in Minā on the eleventh [of Dhū al-Ḥijjah].[68]

3. Spending the night [preceding] the Day of ʿArafah in Minā.

   One performs five [obligatory] prayers in Minā: one leaves Mecca [for Minā] on the Day of *Tarwiyah* [the

---

66 This is according to the Ḥanafīs, Shāfiʿīs and Ḥanbalīs; whereas the Mālikīs have opined that it [*Ṭawāf of* Arrival] is incumbent on anyone who has initiated *iḥrām* from *al-Ḥill*, even if he is from Mecca.

67 An expiation is not incumbent upon him [for missing the *Ṭawāf* of Arrival] according to the Mālikīs if, as a result of performing the *Ṭawāf of* Arrival, he fears missing the standing in ʿArafah.

68 The Shāfiʿīs have opined that it is on the tenth day, and they have added a fourth sermon on the twelfth as a farewell [address] for the pilgrims.

eighth of Dhū al-Ḥijjah] after sunrise and performs in Minā the following prayers: *ẓuhr*, *ʿaṣr*, *maghrib*, *ʿishā* and *fajr*.

4. Spending the night [preceding] the Day of Sacrifice in al-Muzdalifah. This is a sunnah, and what is necessary is to stand in al-Muzdalifah after dawn break [even for a short while].[69]
5. Spending the nights [preceding each of] the Days of *Tashrīq* in Minā: the Days of *Tashrīq* are the eleventh, twelfth and thirteenth of Dhū al-Ḥijjah; it is a sunnah for pilgrims to spend these nights in Minā.[70]

As for the supplementary sunnahs of hajj, i.e. those that supplement other acts, they are many, and there is no need to prolong the discussion by listing them here. They will be mentioned extensively, with the explanation of their ruling, in the exposition of how to perform hajj, if Allah Most High wills.

69 The Mālikīs regard the standing for the duration it takes to unload one's luggage during the night [preceding the Day] of sacrifice in al-Muzdalifah as necessary. As for the Shāfiʿīs and Ḥanbalīs, they consider spending the night in al-Muzdalifah past midnight on the Day of Sacrifice as necessary, and they are in agreement with Mālikīs in that standing in al-Muzdalifah after dawn is a sunnah.

70 Spending these nights in Minā is necessary according to the other three Imams.

2

The Fundamental Rulings of Umrah

Umrah is legally defined as the circumambulation (*ṭawāf*) of the House [Kaaba] and the walk (*sa'y*) between al-Ṣafā and al-Marwah.[71] It is an emphasised sunnah that is to be performed once in a lifetime.[72]

The obligatory acts in umrah

The obligatory acts in umrah are two:

1. *iḥrām*, which is a condition;
2. and the *ṭawāf*, which is an integral.[73]

71 [T] There are many hadiths regarding the merit of umrah, such as the hadith related by Abu Hurayrah that the Messenger of Allah ﷺ said, 'An umrah to umrah is an atonement for what is between them, and an accepted hajj has no reward except Paradise.' (Related by Abū Dāwūd.) 'Itr, Nūr al-Dīn. *al-Ḥajj wa al-'umrah fī al-fiqh al-Islāmī*, 130.

72 This is according to the Ḥanafīs and Mālikīs, whereas according to the more dominant position of the Shāfi'īs and Ḥanbalīs it is necessary once in a lifetime (similar to hajj).

73 The Mālikīs and Ḥanbalīs have additionally included the *sa'y* between al-Ṣafā and al-Marwah. The Shāfi'īs have included the shaving

The necessary acts in umrah

The necessary acts in umrah are also two:

1. *sa'y* (the walk between al-Ṣafā and al-Marwah);
2. and shaving one's head or shortening the hair.[74]

The time for [the validity of performing] umrah lasts throughout the year, though it is recommended in Ramadan because of what the two shaykhs[75] have related on the authority of 'Abd-Allāh ibn 'Abbās ﵄, that the Prophet ﷺ said, 'An umrah in Ramadan is equivalent to a hajj,' and in a narration of Imam Muslim 'it is equivalent to a hajj or [doubt from the narrator] a hajj with me'.

Its performance on the Day of 'Arafah and the four days following it is severely offensive, such that it becomes necessary to offer a sacrifice if performed therein.

Iḥrām for umrah

The method of *iḥrām* for umrah is the same as that for hajj: the intention accompanied by *talbiyah*.[76] One says during the *iḥrām* for umrah,

اَللَّهُمَّ إِنِّيْ أُرِيْدُ الْعُمْرَةَ فَيَسِّرْهَا لِيْ وَتَقَبَّلْهَا مِنِّيْ إِنَّكَ
أَنْتَ السَّمِيْعُ الْعَلِيْمُ . لَبَّيْكَ اللَّهُمَّ لَبَّيْكَ ...

[or shortening one's hair] and observing the order between the performance of the integrals in the above manner.

74 The Mālikīs and the Ḥanbalīs have concurred on the necessity of shaving or cutting the hair.

75 [T] al-Bukhārī and Muslim.

76 Whereas according to the other schools, it is the intention only, as already explained.

O Allah, I intend umrah, so facilitate it for me and accept it from me. Verily, You are the All-Hearing, the All-Knowing. Ever at Your service, ever at Your service...[77]

The sunnahs of *iḥrām* are the same for hajj and umrah, as are the unlawful actions. Similarly, the designated *iḥrām* sites from which a person intending umrah enters *iḥrām* are the same as those from which a person who intends hajj enters *iḥrām*, with one exception, namely whoever is in Mecca or its *Ḥaram* must go to *al-Ḥill* in order to enter *iḥrām*, and that is by consensus of all jurists.

The best area in *al-Ḥill* for entering *iḥrām* for umrah is al-Tanʿīm;[78] it is close to Mecca, and its residential buildings are annexed to it.

The rulings pertaining to the obligatory and necessary acts in umrah are the same as those for hajj; and whatever is sunnah with regard to the obligatory and necessary acts in hajj is also sunnah with regard to umrah; so bear that in mind.

77 [T] It is a sunnah to repeat the *talbiyah* thrice, to invoke blessings and salutations upon the Prophet ﷺ and to supplicate for oneself and others after it. Sirāj al-Dīn, ʿAbd-Allāh. *Manāsik al-ḥajj* [The rites of hajj]. 3rd edn. Aleppo: Dar al-Falāḥ, 1426/2005, 19.

78 The Shāfiʿīs have stated that the best area in *al-Ḥill* to initiate the *iḥrām* for umrah is al-Jiʿrānah, followed by al-Tanʿīm and finally al-Ḥudaybiyyah.

3

The Various Methods of Performing Hajj and Their Legality

Hajj can be performed in three ways or methods that have been established in the authentic Sunnah and over whose validity and legality a consensus has been established. They are:

1. *al-ifrād*: it is for a pilgrim to intend hajj only;
2. *al-qirān*: it is for one to intend in one's *iḥrām* both hajj and umrah simultaneously;
3. and *al-tamattu*ʿ: it is for one to intend umrah only in the months of hajj, and following its completion to exit *iḥrām* and thereafter re-enter the *iḥrām* for hajj.[79]

Therefore, there is no need to further discuss *al-ifrād*, as it is the sole performance of the hajj rites. We shall expound on *al-qirān* and *al-tamattu*ʿ below.

---

79 [T] The one performing hajj according to the method of *al-ifrād* is called a *mufrid*; the one performing it according to the method of *al-qirān* is called a *qārin;* and the one performing it according to the method of *al-tamattu*ʿ is called a *mutamatti*ʿ.

The method of *al-tamattu*ʿ

A *mutamatti*ʿ is a pilgrim coming from outside the designated *iḥrām* sites and who is not a resident of Mecca. This person performs both rites of each pilgrimage completely and individually, which are: firstly, the umrah, for which he enters *iḥrām* from the designated *iḥrām* site, followed by performing its rituals. Thereafter, he proceeds to act in a manner that exits one from the state of *iḥrām* [by shaving his head] and remains in Mecca without *iḥrām*. Secondly, on the Day of *Tarwiyah* (the eighth of Dhū al-Ḥijjah), he enters the *iḥrām* for hajj from Mecca and performs all of its rites; it is, furthermore, necessary for such a person to offer a sacrifice.

The method of *al-qirān*

Al-qirān is for one to enter *iḥrām* for the simultaneous performance of umrah and hajj; thus one says at the point of intending them both,

اَللَّهُمَّ إِنِّيْ أُرِيْدُ الْعُمْرَةَ وَالْحَجَّ فَيَسِّرْهُمَا لِيْ وَتَقَبَّلْهُمَا مِنِّيْ ، إِنَّكَ أَنْتَ
السَّمِيْعُ الْعَلِيْمُ . لَبَّيْكَ اللَّهُمَّ لَبَّيْكَ ، لَبَّيْكَ لَا شَرِيْكَ لَكَ ...

O Allah, I intend umrah and hajj, so facilitate them for me and accept them from me. Verily, You are the All-Hearing, the All-Knowing. Ever at your service, O Allah, ever at your service. Ever at your service; You have no partner ...

Then one performs the rituals for hajj and umrah respectively and does not release oneself from *iḥrām* until the Day of Sacrifice, as we shall explain in detail.

The Ḥanafīs stipulate that a *qārin* initiates *iḥrām for* umrah and hajj simultaneously, just as we have said. Therefore, when he enters Mecca, he begins by circumambulating the house seven times, briskly strutting in the first three, while baring his right shoulder and covering the left (*iḍṭibāʿ*) in all cycles. He then performs the *saʿy* between al-Ṣafā and al-Marwah. These are the rituals for umrah. Thereafter, he begins performing the rituals for hajj: first the seven cycles for the *Ṭawāf of Arrival* (*Ṭawāf al-Qudūm*), followed by the *saʿy* as performed in hajj only (*al-ifrād*). Thus a *qārin* performs two *ṭawāfs* and two *saʿys*: a *ṭawāf* and *saʿy* for umrah and another *ṭawāf* and *saʿy* for hajj.[80]

The sacrificial offering for the completion of *al-tamattuʿ* and *al-qirān*

The scholars agree that it is obligatory for the one performing hajj and umrah individually (*mutamattiʿ*) or together (*qārin*) to make a sacrificial offering.This is due to His Most High's words: *Whoever benefits by his umrah [in drawing near to Allah] up and till [he benefits from performing his] hajj, then [let him sacrifice] whatever offering is feasible for him* [Qur'an 2:196]. It must be of livestock, such as a camel, a cow, a sheep or a goat. Moreover, whatever is conditional

80 As for the other three Imams, they have stated that a *qārin* performs a single *ṭawāf* and saʿ*y*, and this *ṭawāf* and *saʿy* of his suffices for umrah and hajj inclusively: there being no need for repetition. This first *ṭawāf* is the *Ṭawāf of Arrival (Ṭawāf al-Qudūm)*, and the *saʿy* is inclusively the *saʿy* for both the hajj and umrah. One then performs the *Ṭawāf* of the Visit (the obligatory *ṭawāf*) on the Day of Sacrifice, which suffices for both hajj and umrah. If one does not perform the *saʿy* after the *Ṭawāf* of Arrival, then one needs to perform it after the *Ṭawāf* of the Visit.

with respect to the Eid Sacrificial Offering (*al-uḍḥiyyah*) is also applicable here; a sheep or a goat only suffices for a single individual by the consensus of the scholars, whereas a cow or a camel suffices for seven individuals, whether they are from one household or more.[81]

The time of the sacrificial offering for *al-qirān* and *al-tamattuʿ*

The time of the sacrificial offering for *al-qirān* and *al-tamattuʿ* is the Day of Sacrifice, and it lasts from dawn on the Day of Sacrifice until the end of the third day of sacrifice.[82]

The place in which the sacrifice is offered by a *qārin* or a *mutamattiʿ*

The validity of shedding the blood of all sacrificial offerings, apart from the sacrificial offering that is necessary due to

---

81 This is according to the Ḥanafīs, Shāfiʿīs and Ḥanbalīs. The Mālikīs have opined that it is only valid for one household, even if they are more than seven individuals, though invalid for two households, even if they are less than seven individuals; and it is necessary for those contributing in the sacrificial offering (al-*ḥadyī*) and *al-uḍḥiyyah* to distribute [amongst themselves] equally in weight.

82 This is according to the Ḥanafīs, Ḥanbalīs and Mālikīs. The Mālikīs have furthermore allowed for it to be postponed till the end of the month of Dhū al-Ḥijjah. The Shāfiʿīs are of the opinion that it is permissible to sacrifice it when one releases oneself from the *iḥrām* of umrah and whenever one enters *iḥrām* for *al-qirān*, and there is no specific time in which it is necessary for him to sacrifice; thus for the Shāfiʿīs it is akin to the sacrifices that are expiations, i.e. those which are necessary to redress shortcomings within hajj or umrah. However, it is preferable to sacrifice it on the Day of Sacrifice as done by the Prophet ﷺ.

confinement (*al-iḥṣār*),[83] is restricted to *al-Ḥaram*; thus it is invalid to sacrifice any of them outside it by the consensus of the scholars.

It is permissible for a *mutamatti*ʿ or a *qārin* to eat from their sacrificial offering.[84]

The validity of the three methods of hajj

The scholars of the different schools of law have concurred on the validity of each of these methods of hajj which we have expounded, and that whichever of them a Muslim performs, it suffices and is valid. No one has opposed that except a deviant bigot whose aberrations have recently appeared in our times.

The legality of all these three methods of hajj has been explicitly established in the Qur'an and the authentic

---

83 [T] Confinement (*al-iḥṣār*) in Islamic legal terms is when a pilgrim in *iḥrām* is impeded from performing the integrals (the standing in ʿArafah and the *Ṭawāf* of the Visit) of hajj due to an enemy, illness, loss of spending money and so forth; one is therefore obliged to send money to someone in *al-Ḥaram* (according to the Ḥanafīs) for him to slaughter a sheep on one's behalf before one can release oneself from the state of *iḥrām*. According to the Shāfiʿīs and Ḥanbalīs, one can slaughter a sheep at whatever place one is at a standstill, and one is additionally required to shave one's head to release oneself from *iḥrām*, whereas the Mālikīs say that one releases oneself from *iḥrām* by the mere intention to release oneself and is not required to sacrifice or shave; rather, these are sunnah.

84 This is according to the Ḥanafīs, Mālikīs and Ḥanbalīs, because according to them the sacrifice is only necessary as an expression of gratitude [for having completed the rites for both hajj and umrah]. As for the Shāfiʿīs, it is impermissible according to them, because it is a sacrifice offered as an expiation, and so it is similar to the sacrifices which are necessary as atonements for certain violations committed that need to be completely given away in charity.

Sunnah. As for *al-qirān,* then His Most High's words: *And complete hajj and umrah for Allah* [Qur'an 2:196], and His words: *Whoever benefits by his umrah [in drawing near to Allah] up and till [he benefits from performing his] hajj, then [let him sacrifice] whatever offering is feasible for him* [Qur'an 2:196]. So the first verse is unconditional, applicable to all circumstances, because it does not differentiate between one state and another with regard to the *iḥrām* for hajj or umrah and thus proves the legality of all. As for the second verse, it is expressed by His words '*Whoever benefits* (*tamattʿa*)', which proves that there is a pilgrim out there who is not performing *al-tamattuʿ*; hence, it is a proof for the legality of all.

As for the Sunnah, then amongst its evidences is the hadith of ʿĀ'ishah رضي الله عنها, 'We left with the Messenger of Allah ﷺ in the Year of the Farewell Hajj, and there were amongst us those who intended to perform umrah, those who intended to perform hajj and umrah and those who intended to perform hajj [only]...' (An agreed upon narration.)

So, Lady ʿĀ'ishah رضي الله عنها explained that when the Companions had left with the Prophet ﷺ for hajj, there were amongst them those who intended umrah, and these are the *mutamattiʿ*s; those who intended hajj and umrah, and they are the *qārin*s; and those who intended hajj [only], and they are the *mufrid*s. They only did that because of the Prophet ﷺ having taught them to do so, which proves the validity of each method.

As for the consensus on the legality of all the methods, then the actions of the Companions and those after them have been mass-transmitted in [proving] the option between them and that someone in *iḥrām* can choose to do whichever he wishes without condemnation from anyone. The Imams have explicitly stated this consensus: al-Shāfiʿī has said, 'Due to the Book [Qur'an], moreover the Sunnah, and [finally] the fact that I am unaware of any disagreement [between the jurists] regarding it, it is proven that benefiting (*tamattaʿa*) from umrah up and till hajj, performing hajj alone [*al-ifrād*], and *al-qirān* are all valid.'

Similarly, Qāḍī Ḥusayn[85] and Imam al-Nawawī[86] have explicitly stated that there is a consensus on the validity of them all; so there is no justification for claiming that any one of these three methods in particular is obligatory, to the prohibition of the rest.

Which of these types of pilgrimage is best?

There is in the legislation of these three types of pilgrimage, in addition to performing umrah alone, a manifest

85 [T] The Shaykh of the Shāfiʿīs in Khorasān, Abu ʿAlī al-Marwadhī. He studied fiqh under Abu Bakr al-Qaffāl al-Marwadhī. His works include *al-Taʿlīqah* and *al-Fatāwā*; he was given the epithet *Ḥabr al-ummah.* Amongst his students was *Muḥyī al-Sunnah* al-Baghawī; it is also said that *Imām al-Ḥaramayn* al-Juwaynī studied fiqh under him. He died 462 AH in Marw al-Rawdh.

86 [T] *Muḥyī al-Sunnah* Abū Zakariyyā Yaḥyā al-Nawawī, the *ḥāfiẓ* [a hadith master having memorised at least hundred thousand hadiths with their chains of transmission], *faqīh* and the *Shaykh al-Islām* of his time. Born and raised in Nawā, Syria in the year 631 AH. He came to Damascus at a young age to study, at one point studying there for about two years without lying down to sleep. He used to read twelve lessons a day on various Islamic subjects under different scholars. He was known for his asceticism, piety, enjoining good and forbidding evil and miracles. His works are considered the most authoritative in the Shāfiʿī' school, especially his *Minhāj al-ṭālibīn* [The methodology of the seekers]. He returned to Nawā and died there in the year 676 AH at the age of forty-five.

facilitation and an encouragement to repeatedly perform hajj in its various methods. So, if one were to ask which of these types is best, the answer would be that the Imams of Islam have differed regarding that: each method has been preferred by some of the Imams of religion and scholarship, and every school of law is soundly guided. This scholarly difference of opinion gives comfort to the hearts of pilgrims, because each one of them has a basis and an exemplar to follow. Therefore, we regard it best for a pilgrim to consider that which is easier for him and more conducive to engendering presence of heart and humility, as that is a tremendous objective that cannot be ignored.

Important notice regarding the hajj of a woman during menses and lochia

There are numerous case scenarios for these situations, and we shall clarify their ruling in the following cases:

1. a woman enters *iḥrām* for hajj only (*mufridah*) or for hajj and umrah simultaneously (*qārinah*), and her menses or postnatal bleeding impedes her from performing the *ṭawāf*;[87] in this case, she remains [in Mecca without performing *ṭawāf*] until she stands in ʿArafah [on the Day of ʿArafah]. However, she performs the rest of the hajj rites, with the exception of the *ṭawāf* and *saʿy*.[88] Thereafter, when she is in a

87 [T] As she is prohibited from entering the Sacred Mosque, or any mosque for that matter, in this state.

88 [T] Even though the *saʿy* area is not part of the mosque, she is, nevertheless, unable to perform the *saʿy*, as it is only valid after a *ṭawāf*.

state of purity, she performs a single *ṭawāf* and *saʿy* if she is performing hajj only. If, however, she is performing umrah and hajj simultaneously, she has to perform two *ṭawāf*s and two *saʿy*s.[89] In either case, she is not exempt from the Farewell *Ṭawāf* (*Ṭawāf al-Wadāʿ*) by consensus;

2. she initiates the *iḥrām* for umrah and thereafter her menses or postnatal bleeding begins, such that it prevents her from performing umrah before the standing in ʿArafah. If it ceases before it [the standing in ʿArafah], leaving insufficient time for her to purify herself and perform umrah before the *iḥrām* for hajj, she initiates *iḥrām* for hajj (i.e. she intends it and recites the *talbiyah*) and then performs the hajj rituals as mentioned for a women solely performing hajj (*mufridah*). Consequently, by doing this, she has annulled the umrah, and only the hajj is accounted for her. If she then wants to perform an umrah, she intends it after the completion of the hajj rituals;[90]
3. if her menses were to begin during the Days of Sacrifice, after the elapsing of a time sufficient for her to perform the *ṭawāf*, yet because of her menses

---

89 She performs a single *ṭawāf* and *saʿy* according to other than the Ḥanafis, and she is not exempt from the from the Farewell *Ṭawāf* (*Ṭawāf al-Wadāʿ*).

90 As for other than the Ḥanafis, they have opined that her umrah is not annulled; instead, she enters the *iḥrām* for hajj and thus becomes a *qārinah*. The umrah is accounted for her, together with the hajj, and the *ṭawāf* and *saʿy* for hajj suffice her, because according to them a single *ṭawāf* and *saʿy* is sufficient for a *qārinah* for both umrah and hajj, and a sacrificial offering for *al-qirān* is incumbent on her according to them.

she postponed the *Ṭawāf* of Departure (*Ṭawāf al-Ifāḍah*) past its time, then it is necessary for her to offer a sacrifice due to this postponement. If, however, her menses began before or shortly after the Day of Sacrifice, leaving insufficient time to perform the Departure [*ṭawāf*], and consequently her *ṭawāf* is delayed, then no expiation is required of her, nor is she sinful, and that is because of what we know of the Ḥanafī school's position on the necessity (*wujūb*) of performing the *Ṭawāf* of Departure during the Days of Sacrifice;

4. and if her menses began after the standing [in ʿArafah] and the *Ṭawāf* of Departure (*Ṭawāf al-Ifāḍah*), she completes the hajj rites and leaves, and she is exempt from the Farewell *Ṭawāf* (*Ṭawāf al-Wadāʿ*) if she leaves Mecca before she is legally pure by scholarly agreement, with no expiation being required of her for its omission.

4

How to Perform Hajj and Umrah and Their Transmitted Supplications

The first thing you should do when commencing, O pilgrim, is to seek assistance from Allah, asking Him to enable you to perform these rites in the legally required manner and that He opens your heart in observing the appropriate etiquette in those honourable places (*haḍarāt*).

We shall follow here the method of *al-tamattu*ʿ in explaining how to perform the hajj and umrah rituals, as it is easier for the reader to understand than the method of performing umrah or hajj individually. We shall briefly delve into examining the other two types, *al-ifrād* and *al-qirān,* explaining what those performing them require whenever the need arises, in addition to explaining what is appropriate for each and every occasion in terms of etiquette, observations and the supplications that have been transmitted with regards to them.

We have given primary importance to the supplications that have been related from the Prophet ﷺ during the rites of hajj and umrah, and have collected them here in a manner that is rarely paralleled. We have, similarly, cited the most important supplications transmitted from this nation's righteous early community, and have additionally included other transmitted supplications, of a general nature, that are not particular to the rites of hajj and umrah. You should memorise all of these and other supplications, as that will be more effective in evoking greater humility when supplicating, and that you may recollect and supplicate with them at all times, as they are amongst the greatest supplications.

Preparation for the journey to perform hajj or umrah

Know, O pilgrim, this journey of yours is to arrive at and visit the Sacred House of Allah, so prepare for it so as to attain acceptance and that your hopes be reached. Let it begin as a return to Allah and a repentance from all sins and acts of disobedience, redressing wrongs and returning rights to their lawful owners. Do not be deceived by false hopes, visions, dreams and illusions, for it has been established in the hadith 'A martyr is forgiven for every sin except a debt'. Strive in acquiring the expenditure for hajj from pure and lawful earnings as it has also been established in the hadith that 'Indeed, Allah is pure and He only accepts the pure'. Even though one's hajj may be valid and one is absolved of its obligation, there is no reward in it if one's expenditure is not from lawful means. Be eager to accompany a righteous companion, as he would be the best source of assistance on this journey, especially if he is knowledgeable, as he will be an exemplar, a guide and a source of help for one in achieving presence [of heart] and humility.

Recommendations for the journey and its supplications

It is recommended for whoever wants to travel that he visits his family and friends and bids them farewell, and for them to visit and greet him upon his return, just as it is recommended to give charity before a journey, even if it be with something small. The traveller says to those whom he bids farewell that which has been related in the hadith,

أَسْتَوْدِعُكُمُ اللهَ الَّذِيْ لَا تَضِيْعُ وَدَائِعُهُ.

I entrust you to Allah the One whose trusts not neglected.

The resident, in reply to the traveller, says,

أَسْتَوْدِعُ اللهَ دِيْنَكَ وَأَمَانَتَكَ وَخَوَاتِيْمَ عَمَلِك.

I ask Allah that He protect your religion, trust [family and those left behind] and final deeds.

The resident should also request that the traveller pray for him.

It is recommended when departing for a journey to perform two cycles of prayer, reading in them *Sūrah al-Kāfirūn* and *Sūrah al-Ikhlāṣ* together with *Sūrah al-Fātiḥah*. When one leaves one's home for a journey, one should recite the following invocation related in the hadith,

بِسْمِ اللهِ، تَوَكَّلتُ عَلَى اللهِ، وَلَا حَوْلَ وَلَا قُوَّةَ إِلَّا بِاللهِ.

In the name of Allah. I have placed my trust in Allah. There is no strategy or power except through Allah.

Then, when one has set off on the journey, recite that which has been related in the hadith: chant '*Allāhu akbar*' [Allah is the greatest] thrice, followed by reciting,

سُبْحَانَ الَّذِيْ سَخَّرَ لَنَا هٰـذَا وَمَا كُنَّا لَهُ مُقْرِنِيْنَ ، وَإِنَّا إِلَى رَبِّنَا لَـمُنْقَلِبُوْنَ ، اَللَّهُمَّ إِنَّا نَسْأَلُكَ فِيْ سَفرِنَا هٰـذَا الْبِرَّ وَالتَّقْوَى، وَمِنَ الْعَمَلِ مَا تَرْضَى، اَللَّهُمَّ هَوِّنْ عَلَيْنَا سَفَرَنَا هٰـذَا، وَاطْوِ عَنَّا بُعْدَهُ ، اَللَّهُمَّ أَنْتَ الصَّاحِبُ فِي السَّفَرِ وَالْخَلِيْفَةُ فِي الْأَهْلِ، اَللَّهُمَّ إِنِّيْ أَعُوْذُ بِكَ مِنْ وَعْثَاءِ السَّفَرِ وَكَآبَةِ الْـمَنْظَرِ، وَسُوْءِ الْـمُنْقَلَبِ فِي الْـمَالِ وَالْأَهْلِ.

Glory be to the One who has subjugated this [conveyance] for us, as we were [previously] unable to subjugate it. Indeed, to our Lord we are returning. O Allah, we ask You in this journey of ours for all forms of goodness (birr), piety and deeds that are pleasing to You. O Allah, facilitate this journey of ours for us and contract for us its distance. O Allah, You are our companion on this journey and the Guardian we entrust to protect our family. O Allah, I take refuge in You from the arduousness of this journey, distressful incidents [therein] or calamities befalling my wealth and family.

Then recite *Āyah al-Kursī* [the Verse of the Chair], *Sūrah al-Ikhlāṣ* and the Two Protective Chapters (*Sūrah al-Falaq* and *al-Nās*). Constantly remember Allah Most High under all conditions and be eager to perform the prayer at its beginning time; and apart from the legislated dispensations for travelling, beware of neglecting the prayer, since there is nothing equivalent to a single prayer.

Dispensations for a traveller

When you depart, intending a journey of eighty-one kilometres,[91] then know that this journey entitles you to dispensations, beginning from your departure from your city or town and its residential area. These dispensations are:

1. shortening the obligatory prayers consisting of four cycles only.

   These are the afternoon (*ẓuhr*), the late afternoon (*ʿaṣr*) and the nightfall (*ʿishā*) prayers: one prays each of these as two cycles. Shortening [these prayers] is necessary according to the Ḥanafīs.[92] As for the sunset (*maghrib*) and dawn (*fajr*) prayers, one does not shorten them when travelling. The ruling of shortening prayers does not apply to sunnahs, though there is no offence in leaving them during a journey and in praying them in a vehicle; however, it is sunnah to perform them when alighted and settled;[93]

---

91 This is according to the Ḥanafīs, whereas according to others it is eighty-eight and a half kilometres. [T] However, some jurists are of the opinion that it is ninety-five kilometres, which is more prudent.

92 And sunnah according to the other Imams.

93 The other schools have permitted the combining between two prayers as follows: afternoon and late afternoon in one of their respective times, and the sunset and nightfall, likewise as a delayed or early combination. The delayed combination is that one intend at the time of the first prayer, which for instance is the afternoon, to delay it till the late afternoon prayer time; one then performs it at the time of the late afternoon prayer before the late afternoon prayer.

2. non-observance of the Ramadan fast is permissible for someone travelling the distance that allows one to shorten the prayers (*qaṣr*) [i.e. eighty-one kilometres], provided one leaves one's city as a traveller and passes beyond its border before dawn. However, if one leaves after dawn, one is obliged to fast on that day in which one travels, though no longer needs to observe it thereafter during the days one remains a traveller, and this is according to the majority of scholars;[94]
3. one is [legally] considered a traveller, if one stays in a place for a short period, and thus the rulings of travelling apply to one; this duration is fourteen days.[95]

It is preferable that there be no interruption between them, even by a voluntary prayer. One does the same with regards to the sunset prayer.

The early combination is that when one intends the performance of the current prayer, one intends to join the second one to it before its time, and it is valid for one to intend that in one's heart during the performance of the current prayer before the greeting (*salām*); thus one intends to bring forward the late afternoon prayer to the afternoon prayer time and the nightfall to the sunset prayer time; and so one performs the prayer brought forward after the greeting of the current prayer without any interruption between them.

Both combinations, early or delayed, are valid according to the Shāfi'īs and the Ḥanbalīs for a traveller, whereas according to the Mālikīs they are only valid if the journey becomes arduous. It is not valid to combine prayers whilst travelling according to the Ḥanafīs whatsoever, whether delayed or early. Apart from the combinations we have mentioned, nothing else is valid by the consensus of the schools of law; thus it is invalid to combine between the dawn prayer and another prayer, to combine between the afternoon or late-afternoon prayer together with the sunset or nightfall prayer in any situation by consensus; so take heed of that and beware of confusion.

94 The Ḥanbalīs have permitted someone who travels and leaves his city after dawn to break the fast.

95 According to the other three Imams, it is three days excluding the day of entry and departure. So if one alights at a place, intending to stay

Necessary guidelines for safety

As one will be spending a great deal of time during the days of hajj in tents, it is necessary for one to be extra cautious against carelessly doing anything that could cause a fire; otherwise, one would be sinful for whatever afflicts one's self or causes harm to others due to one's negligence. Observe the following guidelines, which are always of the utmost importance, but which require even more consideration during the hajj:

1. do not place inside the tent any substance which is used as fuel, such as Benzene, Kerosene or Butane gas; beware of lighting a fire inside the tent, even with a matchstick, as most fires are from minute sparks, and make sure to blow out matchsticks and cigarette ends and place them in a metal waste bin;
2. when switching on the lights in the tent, make sure the electric wires are closed in completely detached material, that there is no flaying in them, and do not exceed the voltage for a socket;
3. it is necessary to make sure the suitability of electrical appliances to the electric voltage (110 V or 220 V);
4. do not place any electrical cables or extension leads under rugs or under anything on the floor, nor on the flap of the tent;

---

there for four days excluding the two days for entry and departure, one is considered a resident according to the Mālikīs, Shāfiʿīs and Ḥanbalīs; hence, the rulings pertaining to travelling do not apply to him. As for the Ḥanafīs, the least duration for residence (*iqāmah*) in other than one's original place of residence is fifteen days.

5. keep everything away from coming into contact with hot electrical appliances, electrical lamps, irons or heaters. Beware of spreading clothes over electric wires or drying them over the fire;
6. it is necessary to switch off the sockets whenever one leaves the tent or room;
7. close all knobs of a gas stove, likewise the valve of a gas bottle when going to sleep and whenever one leaves the room or tent;
8. keep gas bottles away from any heat source, even the heat of the sun, as that may cause it to explode;
9. if one smells gas or knows that it has escaped, then immediately close the cap of the gas bottle, open the windows of the place and then look for the cause; do not light a fire, a match or turn on a light for fear of an explosion occurring because of the spark from the movement of the electric switch;
10. and keep away from congestion and coming in between large masses of pilgrims, and take advantage of the ample time allocated for each and every rite so that you may perform it after congestion reduces.

How to perform umrah and its supplications

If one is travelling to the designated *iḥrām* site by land or sea, one must prepare for *iḥrām* upon reaching the designated site or when one is parallel with it (if one does not directly pass by it). The ferry blows the horn indicating that one is parallel with the designated site, so as to alert the passengers.

If, however, one is travelling by air, then one should prepare for *iḥrām* either at home or at the airport, by taking off one's stitched clothing and other things that we have mentioned, though without the intention and *talbiyah* until the plane takes off, as the flight may be delayed and therefore inconvenience one due to being bound to the regulations of *iḥrām*. There is no objection in delaying the preparation for *iḥrām* until after the plane has taken off; however, it may expose you to some inconvenience, and you may pass the designated *iḥrām* site without *iḥrām*.

Realise that these laws have been legislated by Allah so that visitors to Mecca do not enter therein except in a state of reverence for the sanctity of the Ancient House, both externally and internally. The correct etiquette includes clipping the nails, cutting the hair for neatness, cleaning the body, shaving the pubic and underarm hair, and taking the sunnah bath for *iḥrām* (which is an emphasised sunnah by consensus, for both men and women, even if a woman is during her lochia or menses).

Then one applies perfume to one's body, but not one's clothing, and wears a lower garment (*izār*) from the naval to below the knee and an upper garment (*ridā*) over one's back and shoulders, both white, washed or new, and wears plastic sandals, so that one may enter *iḥrām* (through intention).

After one has externally prepared oneself, one must turn to the other important preparation, namely the preparation of the heart by imbuing it with awe and reverence, and remembrance of one's departure from this world and that one will be wrapped in shrouds. Then, in this state, turn humbly towards the qiblah and perform the two units of prayer for *iḥrām*, reading *Sūrah al-Kāfirūn* in the first *rak'ah* [after *Sūrah al-Fātiḥah*], and then *Sūrah al-Ikhlāṣ* in the second *rak'ah* [after *Sūrah al-Fātiḥah*]. These two units of prayer are an emphasised sunnah for *iḥrām*. However, do not pray them during the offensive times.[96] One can validly intend the two cycles of prayer for *iḥrām* when performing an obligatory prayer, as with the two cycles of prayer for the greeting of the mosque,[97] and this is by the consensus of all the four schools of law.

Now intend to perform umrah in the heart, because that is the place of one's intention, as one recites with the tongue,

اَللّٰهُمَّ إِنِّيْ أُرِيْدُ الْعُمْرَةَ فَيَسِّرْهَا لِيْ وَتَقَبَّلْهَا مِنِّيْ إِنَّكَ أَنْتَ السَّمِيْعُ الْعَلِيْمُ . لَبَّيْكَ اللّٰهُمَّ لَبَّيْكَ، لَبَّيْكَ لَا شَرِيْكَ لَكَ لَبَّيْكَ ، إِنَّ الْحَمْدَ وَالنِّعْمَةَ لَكَ وَالْمُلْكَ ، لَا شَرِيْكَ لَكَ.

O Allah, I intend umrah, so facilitate it for me and accept it from me. Indeed, You are the All-Hearing, the All-Knowing. Ever at Your service, O Allah, ever at Your service. Ever at Your service, You have no partner, ever at Your service. Indeed, all praise and blessings belong to You, and [likewise] the dominion. You have no partner.[98]

96 [T] According to the Ḥanafis, the offensive prayer times are the following: after dawn; after the *fajr* prayer; at sunrise until twenty minutes after; when the sun is at its zenith; after the ʿ*aṣr* prayer; and after the call for the *maghrib* prayer before its performance.

97 [T] It is recommended to perform two units of prayer when entering a mosque in other than the offensive times, and any prayer performed therein, whether obligatory or sunnah, will account for this prayer, even without the intention to do so.

98 [T] The meaning of *labbayk* is, 'I have answered your call time after time', meaning a perpetual answering. It has been related that

If one intends to perform hajj only (*al-ifrād*), say,

اَللَّهُمَّ إِنِّيْ أُرِيْدُ الْحَجَّ فَيَسِّرْهُ لِيْ وَتَقَبَّلْهُ مِنِّيْ ، إِنَّكَ أَنْتَ السَّمِيْعُ الْعَلِيْمُ. لَبَّيْكَ اللَّهُمَّ لَبَّيْكَ ...

O Allah, I intend hajj, so make it easy for me and accept it from me. Indeed, You are the All-Hearing, the All-Knowing. Ever at Your service, O Allah, ever at Your service ...

However, if one intends to perform umrah and hajj simultaneously (*al-qirān*), recite,

اَللَّهُمَّ إِنِّيْ أُرِيْدُ الْعُمْرَةَ وَالْحَجَّ ...

O Allah, I intend umrah and hajj ...,

followed by chanting the *talbiyah*.

When one has intended and recited the *talbiyah*, one has become a *muḥrim* [someone in the state of *iḥrām*], having commenced the act of worship by intention and absorbed in the sanctity of this great act of obedience, all for the sake of Allah Most High. Therefore, be conscious and mindful of Him, in public and private, and count every action against oneself and hold it accountable: in words, even if they be few and brief, and actions, even if they be habitual. Exercise patience, spend wealth and exhibit good character as a means [of attaining the goal], as these are necessary on a journey, especially the journey for hajj.

---

whoever enters *iḥrām* (*muḥrim*) mentions in the *talbiyah* that for which he is entering *iḥrām*; so he says, 'Ever at Your service, O Allah, ever at Your service. Ever at Your service for umrah,' for example, or 'for hajj,' or 'for umrah and hajj,' and then he completes the *talbiyah*.

Profusely and constantly chant the *talbiyah* with a medium pitched voice during all occasions, whether standing or sitting, walking or riding, alighting or travelling, change of circumstances, whether in time or place, such as the coming of the night or day, during the last parts of the night, when meeting and departing, after prayers and in mosques. One should not omit anything of the *talbiyah*, though if one adds to it, then that is permissible.

Amongst the additions that have been transmitted regarding the *talbiyah* are:

لَبَّيْكَ إِلَـٰهَ الْحَقِّ لَبَّيْكَ.

Ever at Your service, [You are] the Real God,
ever at Your service.

لَبَّيْكَ إِنَّ الْعَيْشَ عَيْشُ الْآخِرَةِ.

Ever at Your service. Surely the [real] life
is the life of the next world.

لَبَّيْكَ، لَبَّيْكَ وَسَعْدَيْكَ ، والْخَيْرُ بِيَدَيْكَ ،
لَبَّيْكَ وَالرَّغْبَاءُ إِلَيْكَ وَالْعَمَلُ.

Ever at Your service, ever at Your service and
ready to please You with obedience to You, and
all goodness is in Your hands [i.e. power]. Ever at
Your service, and [our] beseeching is to You
and [likewise our] deeds [are for You].

لَبَّيْكَ ذَا النَّعْمَـاءِ وَالْفَضْلِ الْحَسَنِ.

Ever at Your service, O Possessor of favours and beautiful grace.

لَبَّيْكَ حَقّاً حَقّاً ، تَعَبُّداً وَرِقّـاً.

Truly ever at Your service and truly in worship and slavehood [to You].

Conclude the *talbiyah* by supplicating, asking Allah Most High for His pleasure and forgiveness, taking refuge in His mercy from the Fire and invoking blessings upon the Prophet ﷺ, and repeat the supplication on every occasion three times in emulation of the Sunnah.

Entering Mecca

When one approaches the Ennobled Mecca, know that around it is the Sacred Precinct (*al-Ḥaram*), whose game is unlawful [for hunting] under all circumstances, as is cutting its trees which were not purposely grown for cutting and plucking, and the one who enters it is safe. When one reaches the precinct of *al-Ḥaram*, recite:

اَللَّهُمَّ هَـٰذَا حَرَمُكَ وَأَمْنُكَ ، فَحَرِّمْنِي عَلَى النَّارِ، وَأَمِّنِّيْ عَذَابَكَ يَوْمَ تَبْعَثُ عِبَادَكَ ، وَاجْعَلْنِيْ مِنْ أَوْلِيَائِكَ وَأَهْلِ طَاعَتِكَ.

O Allah, this is Your Sacred Precinct and Your sanctuary, so make me forbidden for the Fire, save me from Your torment on the day You resurrect Your slaves, and make me amongst Your friends and obedient ones.

And pray for whatever one wishes, for oneself and for whomever one wishes.

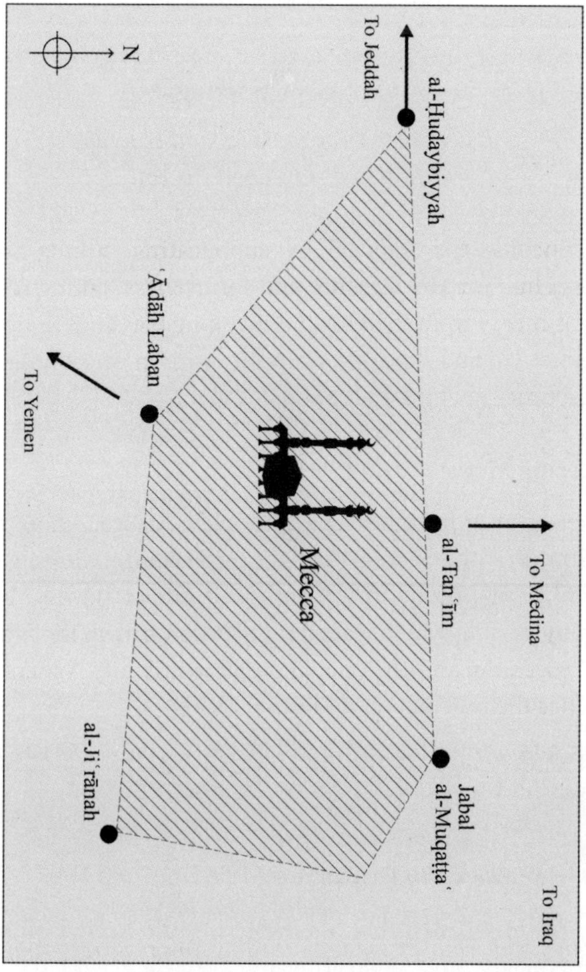

Figure 2: The Sacred Precinct (*al-Ḥaram*) and its borders and points of exit and entry.

It is recommended that one alight before entering Mecca at Dhū Ṭuwā, en-route to the Mosque of ʿĀ'ishah, or at any other place if it is convenient for one, and take a bath to enter Mecca.

When one enters Mecca, recite the supplication transmitted from the Prophet ﷺ for entering it,

اَللَّهُمَّ الْبَلَدُ بَلَدُكَ ، وَالْبَيْتُ بَيْتُكَ ، جِئْتُ أَطْلَبُ رَحْمَتَكَ ، وَأَؤُمُّ طَاعَتَكَ ، مُتَّبِعاً لِأَمْرِكَ ، رَاضِياً بِقَدَرِكَ ، مُسَلِّماً لِأَمْرِكَ، أَسْأَلُكَ مَسْأَلَةَ الْمُضْطَرِّ إِلَيْكَ الْمُشْفِقِ مِنْ عَذَابِكَ أَنْ تَسْتَقْبِلَنِيْ بِعَفْوِكَ ، وَأَنْ تَتَجَاوَزَ عَنِّيْ بِرَحْمَتِكَ ، وَ أَنْ تُدْخِلَنِيْ جَنَّتَكَ.

O Allah, the city is Your city, and the House is Your House. I have come, seeking Your mercy, intending obedience to You, complying with Your commandment, content with Your apportionment and surrendering to Your command. I ask You as the one who is in dire need of You asks You, the one who is fearful of Your torment, that You receive me with Your pardon, excuse me out of Your mercy and allow me to enter Your garden.

Moreover, praise and extol Allah as He deserves and invoke blessings upon the Elect Prophet ﷺ.

Entering the Sacred Mosque

It is recommended that one hasten to the Sacred Mosque immediately after depositing one's luggage with the hajj guide [or at the Hotel]. So enter the Mosque from the Door of *Salām* if one is nearby and recite that which is generally recommended when entering mosques: invoking blessings and peace upon the Prophet ﷺ, followed by reciting,

رَبِّ اغْفِرْ لِيْ ذُنُوْبِيْ وَافْتَحْ لِيْ أَبْوَابَ رَحْمَتِكَ.

My Lord, forgive me my sins and open for me the doors to Your mercy.

When one leaves the mosque, invoke blessings upon the Prophet ﷺ and recite,

رَبِّ اغْفِرْ لِيْ ذُنُوْبِيْ وَافْتَحْ لِيْ أَبْوَابَ فَضْلِكَ.

My Lord, forgive me my sins and open for me the doors to Your bounty.

Recite after entering the Sacred Mosque,

اَللَّهُمَّ إِنَّ هٰـذَا حَرَمُكَ وَمَوْضِعُ أَمْنِكَ فَحَرِّمْ لَحْمِيْ ، وَبَشَرِيْ ، وَدَمِيْ ، وَمُخِّيْ ، وَعِظَامِيْ عَلَى النَّارِ.

O Allah, this is Your Sacred Precinct and Your sanctuary, so make forbidden my flesh, my skin, my blood, my marrow and my bones for the Fire.

When one's gaze falls on the Kaaba, try to muster as much humility, self-abasement, subservience, awe and reverence as possible, for this is the hallmark of the righteous and the gnostic slaves of Allah, because beholding the House inspires one to yearn for the Lord of the House.

It is recommended that one supplicate upon seeing the Kaaba, as this is amongst the places wherein prayers are answered, and recite,

اَللَّهُمَّ زِدْ هَـٰذَا الْبَيْتَ تَشْرِيْفاً وَتَكْرِيْماً، وَتَعْظِيْماً وَمَهَابَةً، وَزِدْ مَنْ شَرَّفَهُ وَ كَرَّمَهُ، مِمَّنْ حَجَّهُ وَاعْتَمَرَهُ تَشْرِيْفاً وَتَعْظِيْماً وَبِرّاً.

O Allah, increase this House in honour and ennoblement, reverence and awe, and increase the one who honours and ennobles it, of those who travel to it for hajj and umrah, in honour, reverence and piety.

اَللَّهُمَّ أَنْتَ السَّلَامُ، وَمِنْكَ السَّلَامُ، فَحَيِّنَا رَبَّنَا بِالسَّلَامِ.

O Allah, You are al-Salām,[99] *and from You is peace, so give us life, our Lord, in the Abode of Peace.*

Then invoke blessings upon the Prophet ﷺ, because it is one of the most important invocations, and supplicate with whatever formulae you wish and with this particular supplication of some of the scholars,

اَللَّهُمَّ إِنِّيْ عَبْدُكَ وَزَائِرُكَ وَعَلَى كُلِّ مَزُوْرٍ حَقٌّ ، وَأَنْتَ خَيْرُ مَزُوْرٍ، فَأَسْأَلُكَ أَنْ تَغْفِرَ لِيْ وَتَرْحَمَنِيْ ، وَتَفُكَّ رَقَبَتِيْ مِنَ النَّارِ.

O Allah, I am Your slave and visitor, and upon every host there is a right, and You are the best Host, so I ask You to forgive me, have mercy on me and unfetter my neck from the Fire.

Circumambulation [*Ṭawāf*]

It is sunnah to hasten to perform the *ṭawāf*, so intend to circumambulate the House immediately, as it is the greeting

99 [T] One of the names of Allah Most High; it means the One who is free from all blemishes or the One who gives peace and security.

of the *Ḥaram* [Mosque]. This *ṭawāf* accounts for the *ṭawāf* of umrah for whoever intends umrah and likewise for whoever intends both hajj and umrah simultaneously (*qārin*), though the one combining between hajj and umrah is also required to perform another *ṭawāf* for Arrival and another *sa ʿy* for hajj. As for someone who intends hajj only (*mufrid*), then it accounts for the *Ṭawāf* of Arrival (*Ṭawāf al-Qudūm*); hence, it is a sunnah to intend the required *ṭawāf*. Cease chanting the *talbiyah* when you begin the *ṭawāf*, and when you enter the *ṭawāf* area (*maṭāf*) within the mosque, recite,

رَبِّ أَدْخِلْنِي مُدْخَلَ صِدْقٍ ، وَأَخْرِجْنِي مُخْرَجَ صِدْقٍ ،
وَاجْعَل لِّي مِنْ لَدُنْكَ سُلْطَاناً نَصِيْراً.

My Lord, enable me to enter sincerely, and enable me to exit sincerely, and bring forth for me from Yourself a conclusive proof.

Then place the middle of the upper garment under the right armpit and its two ends over one's left shoulder (*iḍṭibāʿ*), and turn towards the Black Stone so that one passes by it with one's entire body as one heads towards the Yemeni corner. Then turn and face the [Black] Stone and touch it (*istilām*) by placing one's hands on it and one's face in between one's palms, followed by kissing and prostrating on it to Allah Most High.

Whenever one encounters congestion, avoid causing inconvenience; rather; confine oneself to pointing to the Stone with one's hands, as inconveniencing people is unlawful and obligatory for one to avoid, whilst touching the Stone is a sunnah, and it is not permissible to commit an unlawful act for the sake of a sunnah.

The manner of pointing is that one raise one's hands parallel to one's shoulders and turn one's palms towards the Black Stone, pointing them towards it. There is, in that, a reminder of Allah's taking the pledge of allegiance from His slaves to obey Him, so resolve to fulfil that, because whoever breaches it is deserving of [divine] wrath, and we take refuge in Allah. Invoke blessings upon the Prophet ﷺ, and begin with the *ṭawāf*, briskly strutting in the first three cycles only. It is a sunnah, for men only, to bare the right shoulder and cover the left and briskly strut in every *ṭawāf* after which there is a *saʿy*.

Imagine, when strutting, that you are fleeing from this world to take refuge in the Real [Allah] Most High, and supplicate for whatever good you want in this world and the next: for yourself, for those whom you love and for the Muslims [in general]. Profusely supplicate and exert yourself in pleading to Allah, because the *ṭawāf* is one of the occasions wherein supplications are answered.[100]

Thereafter, touch and kiss the Black Stone whenever you pass by it, or point to it [if unable to kiss it], followed by touching the Yemeni corner, which is the corner before the

---

100 [T] 'It is related from Ḥasan [al-Baṣrī] ؓ , "Supplications are answered therein [during hajj] on fifteen occasions: during *ṭawāf*, at the Multazam, under the rain pipe (*mīzāb*), in the House [Kaaba], at the Zamzam well [or when drinking its water], on al-Ṣafā and al-Marwah, in the *saʿy* area, behind the *Maqām* [of Ibrāhīm], in ʿArafāt, al-Muzdalifah, Minā and at the three sites (*Jamarāt*)." Thus deprived is the one who does not strive in supplicating therein.' al-Nawawī, Yaḥyā Sharaf. *al-Adhkār* [The invocations]. Dār al-Minhāj. 1st edn.1425/2005, 328.

corner in which is the Black Stone; however, it is not, by consensus, a sunnah to kiss or prostrate on it, nor to point to it when unable to kiss it.[101]

The supplications for *ṭawāf*[102]

It is recommended that one recite at the beginning of the *ṭawāf* and whenever one touches or passes by the Stone,

بِسْمِ اللهِ، وَ اللهُ أَكْبَرُ، اَللَّهُمَّ إِيْمَـاناً بِكَ ، وَتَصْدِيْقاً بِكِتَابِكَ ،
وَوَفَاءً بِعَهْدِكَ ، وَاتِّبَاعاً لِسُنَّةِ نَبِيِّكَ.

In the name of Allah. Allah is the greatest. O Allah, out of faith in You, conviction in Your book, in fulfilment of Your covenant and in emulation of Your Prophet's Sunnah ﷺ.

And supplicate between the Yemeni corner and the Black Stone corner with this supplication of the Prophet ﷺ,

---

101 This is according to the Ḥanafīs and Mālikīs, while according to the Shāfiʿīs and Ḥanbalīs one points to it if one is unable to kiss it.

102 [T] 'The distribution of supplications over the cycles of *ṭawāf* and *saʿy* has not been established in the Sunnah; rather, it is merely the preference of the scholars to facilitate matters for the pilgrim and remind one of those meanings with which to supplicate; and I have followed their footsteps and selected these supplications from the noble Qur'an and from the book *al-Ibtihāj bi adhkār al-musāfir al-ḥājj* [The joy by the invocations of the traveller pilgrim] by *al-Ḥafiẓ* al-Sakhāwi (66-71), and the book *Adʿiyyah al-ḥajj wa al-ʿumrah* [The supplications for hajj and umrah] by *ʿAllāmah* Quṭb al-Dīn al-Ḥanafī (85-90).' ʿItr, Nūr al-Dīn. *al-Ḥajj wa al-ʿumrah fī al-fiqh al-Islāmī*, 209.

رَبَّنَا آتِنَا فِي الدُّنْيَا حَسَنَةً وَفِي الْآخِرَةِ حَسَنَةً وَقِنَا عَذَابَ النَّارِ.

O our Lord, give us good in this world and good in the next world, and guard us from the torment of the Fire.

This was the most oft-repeated supplication of the Prophet ﷺ on most occasions, so profusely recite it.

Moreover, the Prophet ﷺ would also supplicate between the two corners,

رَبِّ قَنِّعْنِي بِمَا رَزَقْتَنِيْ وَبَارِكْ لِيْ فِيْهِ ، وَاخْلُفْ
عَلَيَّ كُلَّ غَائِبَةٍ لِيْ بِخَيْرٍ.

O my Lord, make me content with what You have given me as sustenance, grant me blessings therein and grant me that which is better than what I have lost.

Constantly recite these supplications in every cycle. It is also virtuous to complete a recital of the Qur'an in one's *ṭawāf*s, but read with a low-pitched voice. Furthermore, profusely invoke blessings upon the one who was sent as a mercy to all the worlds, upon him be the best of blessings and salutations, during the *ṭawāf*. Supplicate for whatever you want of the good things in this world and in your religion. It is better for one to supplicate from memory, because it is more effective in humbling the heart.

Hereunder are supplications divided appropriately for each cycle of the *ṭawāf*, which one may recite in addition to the supplications mentioned previously, those for the *saʿy* and whatever else one chooses to recite.

The first cycle of the ṭawāf

سُبْحَانَ اللّٰـهِ ، وَالْحَمْدُ لِلّٰـهِ ، وَلَا إِلَهَ إِلَّا اللّٰـهُ ، وَ اللّٰـهُ أَكْبَرُ،
وَلَا حَوْلَ وَلا قُوَّةَ إِلَّا بِاللّٰـهِ الْعَلِيِّ الْعَظِيْمِ.

Glory be to Allah. All praise is due to Allah. There is no god except Allah. Allah is the greatest. There is no strategy or power except through Allah Most High, the Great.

اَللَّهُمَّ إِنَّ هَـٰذَا الْبَيْتَ بَيْتُكَ ، وَالْحَرَمَ حَرَمُكَ ، وَهَـٰذَا مَقَامُ
الْعَائِذِ بِكَ مِنَ النَّارِ، فَحَرِّمْ لَحْمِيْ وَبَشَرِيْ عَلَى النَّارِ.

O Allah, verily this House is Your House; the Sacred Precinct is Your Sacred Precinct; and this is where the one taking refuge in You from the Fire stands, so make forbidden my flesh and my skin for the Fire.

اَللَّهُمَّ إِنِّيْ أَسْأَلُكَ الْعَفْوَ وَالْعَافِيَةَ وَالْـمُعَافَاةَ الدَّائِمَةَ فِي الدِّيْنِ
وَالدُّنْيَا وَالْآخِرَةِ ، وَالْفَوْزَ بِالْجَنَّةِ وَالنَّجَاةَ مِنَ النَّارِ.

O Allah, I ask You for pardon, well-being, perpetual protection in religion, in this world and the next, attainment of Paradise and salvation from the Fire.

اَللَّهُمَّ اجْعَلْهُ حَجّاً مَبْرُوْراً ، وَسَعْياً مَشْكُوْراً ، وَذَنْباً مَغْفُوْراً ،
اَللَّهُمَّ لَا إِلَهَ إِلَّا أَنْتَ ، وَأَنْتَ تُحْيِيْ بَعْدَ مَا أَمَتَّ.

O Allah, make it an accepted pilgrimage, a rewarded endeavour and [my sin] a forgiven sin. O Allah, there is no deity except You, and You bring back to life after You cause death.

The second cycle of the ṭawāf

اَللَّهُمَّ يَسِّرْ لِيَ الْآخِرَةَ وَالْأُوْلَى ، وَاعْصِمْنِيْ بِأَلْطَافِكَ ،
وَاجْعَلْنِيْ مِمَّنْ يُحِبُّكَ وَيُحِبُّ رَسُوْلَكَ وَمَلَائِكَتَكَ ، وَيُحِبُّ
عِبَادَكَ الصَّالِحِيْنَ ، وَأَوْلِيَاءَكَ الْـمُتَّقِيْنَ.

O Allah, make easy for me the latter life and the former, protect me with Your subtle kindnesses and make me from amongst those who love You, love Your Messenger and angels and love Your righteous servants and God-conscious friends.

اَللَّهُمَّ رَبَّنَا لَا تَجْعَلْنَا فِتْنَةً لِلْقَوْمِ الظَّالِـمِيْنَ ، وَنَجِّنَا
بِرَحْمَتِكَ مِنَ الْقَوْمِ الْكَافِرِيْنَ.

O Allah, our Lord, subject us not to a trial [of defeat] to [tempt] the wrongdoing people [to exult in their unbelief],[103] *and save us by Your mercy from the disbelieving folk.*

اَللَّهُمَّ إِنَّ هَـٰذَا الْبَيْتَ بَيْتُكَ ، وَالْحَرَمَ حَرَمُكَ ، وَالْأَمْنَ أَمْنُكَ،
وَالْعَبْدَ عَبْدُكَ ، وَأَنَا عَبْدُكَ وَابْنُ عَبْدِكَ ، وَهَـٰذَا مَقَامُ الْعَائِذِ

---

103 [Ed] The middle section of this translation was taken from Hammad, Ahmad Zaki. *The Glorious Quran: A Modern-Phrased Interpretation in English*. Lucent Interpretations 2009, 357.

بِكَ مِنَ النَّارِ، فَحَرِّمْ لُـحُوْمَنَا وَبَشَرَتَنَا عَلَى النَّارِ. اَللَّهُمَّ حَبِّبْ إِلَيْنَا الْإِيْمَـانَ وَزَيِّنْهُ فِيْ قُلُوْبِنَا ، وَكَرِّهْ إِلَيْنَا الْكُفْرَ وَالْفُسُوْقَ وَالْعِصْيَانَ، وَاجْعَلْنَا مِنَ الرَّاشِدِيْنَ ، اَللَّهُمَّ قِنِيْ عَذَابَكَ يَوْمَ تَبْعَثُ عِبَادَكَ ، اَللَّهُمَّ ارْزُقْنِيَ الْجَنَّةَ بِغَيْرِ حِسَابٍ.

O Allah, verily this House is Your House; the Sacred Precinct is Your Sacred Precinct; the Sanctuary is Your Sanctuary; the slave is Your slave, and I am Your slave, the son of Your slave; and this is where the one who takes refuge in You from the Fire stands, so make forbidden our flesh and skin for the Fire. O Allah, make beloved to us faith, and beautify it in our hearts, and make loathsome to us disbelief, impiety and disobedience, and make us amongst the rightly guided. O Allah, guard me from Your torment on the day You resurrect Your slaves. O Allah, grant me Paradise without reckoning.

اَللَّهُمَّ إِنِّيْ أَسْأَلُكَ مِنَ الْخَيْرِ كُلِّهِ عَاجِلِهِ وَآجِلِهِ مَا سَأَلَكَ عَبْدُكَ وَرَسُوْلُكَ مُحَمَّدٌ ﷺ ، وَأَعُوْذُ بِكَ مِنَ الشَّرِ كُلِّهِ عَاجِلِهِ وَآجِلِهِ مَا اسْتَعَاذَكَ مِنْهُ عَبْدُكَ وَرَسُوْلُكَ مُحَمَّدٌ ﷺ.

O Allah, verily I ask You for all kinds of goodness—its immediate and delayed—for which Your servant and Messenger Muhammad ﷺ asked You, and I take refuge in You from all evil—its immediate and delayed—from which Your servant and Messenger Muhammad ﷺ took refuge in You.

اَللَّهُمَّ اجْعَلْهُ حَجّاً مَبْرُوْراً ، وَسَعْياً مَشْكُوْراً ، وَذَنْباً مَغْفُوْراً .
اَللَّهُمَّ لَا إِلَهَ إِلَّا أَنْتَ وَأَنْتَ تُحْيِيْ بَعْدَ مَا أَمَتَّ.

O Allah, make it an accepted pilgrimage, a rewarded endeavour and [my sin] a forgiven sin. O Allah, there is no deity except You, and You bring back to life after You cause death.

The third cycle of the ṭawāf

اَللَّهُمَّ إِنِّيْ أَعُوْذُ بِكَ مِنَ الشَكِّ وَالشِّرْكِ ، وَالشِّقَاقِ وَالنِّفَاقِ،
وَسُوْءِ الأَخْلَاقِ ، وَسُوْءِ الْمُنْقَلَبِ فِي الْمَالِ وَالْأَهْلِ وَالْوَلَدِ.

O Allah, I take refuge in You from doubt, associating [partners with You], discord, hypocrisy, bad character and misfortune [afflicting my] wealth, family and children.

اَللَّهُمَّ إِنِّيْ أَعُوْذُ بِكَ مِنَ الْكُفْرِ وَالْفَقْرِ، وَمِنْ مَوَاقِفِ
الْخِزْيِ فِي الدُّنْيَا وَالآخِرَةِ.

O Allah, I take refuge in You from disbelief, poverty and from any humiliation in this world and the next.

اَللَّهُمَّ إِنِّيْ أَسْأَلُكَ رِضَاكَ وَالْجَنَّةَ ، وَأَعُوْذُ بِكَ مِنْ سَخَطِكَ وَالنَّارِ،
وَأَعُوْذُ بِكَ مِنْ جَمِيْعِ الْمَضَالِّ وَالْمَضَارِّ فِي الْآخِرَةِ وَهَٰذِهِ الدَّارِ.

O Allah, I ask You for Your pleasure and Paradise, and I take refuge in You from Your wrath and the Fire, and I take refuge in You from all forms of misguidance and harm in the next life and in this abode.

اَللَّهُمَّ إِنِّيْ أَعُوْذُ بِكَ مِنْ عَذَابِ النَّارِ، وَعَذَابِ الْقَبْرِ ، وَأَعُوْذُ بِكَ مِنْ فِتْنَةِ الْـمَحْيَا وَالْـمَمَـاتِ ، وَأَعُوْذُ بِكَ مِنْ فِتْنَةِ الْـمَسِيْحِ الدَّجَّالِ.

O Allah, I take refuge in You from the torment of the Fire and the torment of the grave, and I take refuge in You from the tribulation of life and death, and I take refuge in You from the tribulation of the False Messiah.

اَللَّهُمَّ اجْعَلْهُ حَجّاً مَبْرُوْراً ، وَسَعْياً مَشْكُوْراً ، وَذَنْباً مَغْفُوْراً ، اَللَّهُمَّ لَا إِلٰـهَ إِلَّا أَنْتَ ، وَأَنْتَ تُحْيِيْ بَعْدَ مَا أَمَتَّ.

O Allah, make it an accepted pilgrimage, a rewarded endeavour and [my sin] a forgiven sin. O Allah, there is no deity except You, and You bring back to life after You cause death.

The fourth cycle of the ṭawāf

اَللَّهُمَّ أَظِلَّنِيْ تَحْتَ ظِلِّ عَرْشِكَ يَوْمَ لَا ظِلَّ إِلَّا ظِلُّكَ ، وَلَا بَاقٍ إِلَّا وَجْهُكَ الْكَرِيْمُ.

O Allah, shade me under the shade of Your throne on that day when there shall be no shade except Your shade and nothing shall remain except Your noble countenance [i.e. being].

يَا عَالِمَ مَا فِي الصُّدُوْرِ، أَخْرِجْنِيْ يَا اللهُ مِنَ الظُّلُمَـاتِ إِلَى النُّوْرِ.

O Knower of what the hearts contain, bring me out, O Allah, from darkness to light.

اَللَّهُمَّ احْشُرْنِيْ تَحْتَ لِوَاءِ سَيِّدِ الْـمُرْسَلِيْنَ ، وَاسْقِنِيْ
مِنْ حَوْضِهِ شَرْبَةً لَا أَظْمَأُ بَعْدَهُ أَبَداً.

O Allah, gather me under the banner of the Master of the Messengers, Muhammad ﷺ, and give me a drink from his basin after which I shall never be thirsty.

اَللَّهُمَّ أَدْخِلْنِيَ الْجَنَّةَ بِغَيْرِ عَذَابٍ وَلَا حِسَابٍ ، وَارْزُقْنِيْ
مُرَافَقَةَ نَبِيِّكَ سَيِّدِنَا مُحَمَّدٍ ﷺ فِيْ أَعْلَى جَنَّةِ الْخُلْدِ.

O Allah, allow me to enter Paradise without torment or accountability, and grant me the company of Your Prophet, our master Muhammad ﷺ, in the loftiest Paradise of Eternity.

اَللَّهُمَّ إِنِّيْ أَسْأَلُكَ مُوْجِبَاتِ رَحْمَتِكَ ، وَعَزَائِمَ مَغْفِرَتِكَ ،
وَالسَّلَامَةَ مِنْ كُلِّ إِثْمٍ ، وَالْغَنِيْمَةَ مِنْ كُلِّ بِرٍّ،
وَالْفَوْزَ بِالْجَنَّةِ وَالنَّجَاةَ مِنَ النَّارِ.

O Allah, I ask You for deeds that necessitate Your mercy, deeds that ensure Your forgiveness, safety from every sin, effortless attainment of every good, attainment of Paradise and salvation from the Fire.

رَبِّ اغْفِرْ وَارْحَمْ ، وَاعْفُ عَمَّا تَعْلَمُ ، وَأَنْتَ الْأَعَزُّ الْأَكْرَمُ.

My Lord, forgive, have mercy and pardon [us] of what You know. You are the Mightiest, the Most Generous.

The fifth cycle of the ṭawāf

اَللَّهُمَّ يَا وَاجِدُ يَا مَاجِدُ ، لَا تُزِلْ عَنِّيْ نِعْمَةً أَنْعَمْتَ بِهَا عَلَيَّ ،
وَأَعِذْنِيْ رَبِّ مِنْ تَحَوُّلِ عَافِيَتِكَ ، وَجَمِيعِ سَخَطِكَ.

O Allah, O Self-Sufficient One, O Glorious One, do not divest me of a blessing that You have bestowed upon me, and give me refuge, my Lord, from losing Your protection and from all [forms] of Your wrath.

رَبَّنَا لَا تُزِغْ قُلُوْبَنَا بَعْدَ إِذْ هَدَيْتَنَا، وَهَبْ لَنَا مِنْ
لَدُنْكَ رَحْمَةً ، إِنَّكَ أَنْتَ الْوَهَّابُ.

Our Lord, do not deviate our hearts after having guided us, and grant us from Yourself a mercy. Verily, You are the Benevolent.

رَبِّ أَوْزِعْنِيْ أَنْ أَشْكُرَ نِعْمَتَكَ الَّتِيْ أَنْعَمْتَ عَلَيَّ وَعَلَى
وَالِدَيَّ ، وَأَنْ أَعْمَلَ صَالِحاً تَرْضَاهُ ، وَأَصْلِحْ لِيْ فِيْ ذُرِّيَّتِيْ ،
إِنِّيْ تُبْتُ إِلَيْكَ وَإِنِّيْ مِنَ الْمُسْلِمِيْنَ.

My Lord, inspire me to show gratitude for the blessings that You have bestowed upon me and my parents, and [inspire me] to do righteous deeds that please You, and make righteous my progeny. I have repented to You and I am from amongst the Muslims.

اَللَّهُمَّ إِنِّيْ أَسْأَلُكَ مِنْ خَيْرِ مَا سَأَلَكَ مِنْهُ نَبِيُّكَ سَيِّدُنَا مُحَمَّدٌ ﷺ
وَأَعُوْذُ بِكَ مِنْ شَرِّ مَا اسْتَعَاذَكَ مِنْهُ نَبِيُّكَ سَيِّدُنَا مُحَمَّدٌ ﷺ.

O Allah, I ask You for the best of what Your Prophet, our master Muhammad ﷺ, asked You, and I take refuge in You from the worst of what Your Prophet our master Muhammad ﷺ, took refuge in You.

اَللَّهُمَّ إِنِّيْ أَسْأَلُكَ الْجَنَّةَ وَمَا يُقَرِّبُ إِلَيْهَا مِنْ قَوْلٍ أَوْ عَمَلٍ ، وَأَعُوْذُ بِكَ مِنَ النَّارِ وَمَا يُقَرِّبُ إِلَيْهَا مِنْ قَوْلٍ أَوْ عَمَلٍ.

O Allah, I ask You for Paradise and those words and deeds that bring one near to it, and I take refuge in You from the Fire and those words and deeds that bring one near to it.

رَبِّ اغْفِرْ وَارْحَمْ ، وَاعْفُ عَمَّـا تَعْلَمُ ، وَأَنْتَ الْأَعَزُّ الْأَكْرَمُ.

My Lord, forgive, have mercy and pardon [us] of what You know. You are the Mightiest, the Most Generous.

The sixth cycle of the ṭawāf

اَللَّهُمَّ رَبَّنَا آتِنَا مِنْ لَدُنْكَ رَحْمَةً ، وَهَيِّءْ لَنَا مِنْ أَمْرِنَا رَشَداً.

O Allah, our Lord, grant us from Yourself a mercy, and facilitate for us direction in our affair.

اَللَّهُمَّ رَبَّنَا هَبْ لَنَا مِنْ أَزْوَاجِنَا وَذُرِّيَّاتِنَا قُرَّةَ أَعْيُنٍ وَاجْعَلْنَا لِلْمُتَّقِيْنَ إِمَاماً.

O Allah, our Lord, grant us happiness from our spouses and progeny, and make us a leader for the God-conscious.

اَللَّهُمَّ إِنَّ لَكَ عَلَيَّ حُقُوْقاً كَثِيْرَةً فِيْمَـا بَيْنِيْ وَبَيْنَكَ ، وَحُقُوْقاً كَثِيْرَةً فِيْمَـا بَيْنِيْ وَبَيْنَ خَلْقِكَ. اَللَّهُمَّ مَا كَانَ لَكَ مِنْهَا فَاغْفِرْهُ لِيْ ، وَمَا كَانَ لِخَلْقِكَ فَتَحَمَّلْهُ عَنِّيْ يَا أَرْحَمَ الرَّاحِمِيْنَ.

O Allah, verily You have many rights over me that are between me and You, and many rights that are between me and Your creation; O Allah, whatever of them [the rights] belongs to You, then forgive me for it, and whatever of them belongs to Your creation, then bear it on my behalf, O Most Merciful of the Merciful.

اَللَّهُمَّ إِنَّ وَجْهَكَ كَرِيْمٌ ، وَبَيْتَكَ عَظِيْمٌ ، وَأَنْتَ يَا اللهُ ، حَلِيْمٌ كَرِيْمٌ عَظِيْمٌ تُحِبُّ الْعَفْوَ، فَاعْفُ عَنِّيْ.

O Allah, verily Your countenance is noble; Your House is great, and You, O Allah, are forbearing, generous and great; You love [those who] pardon, so pardon me.

رَبِّ اغْفِرْ وَارْحَمْ ، وَاعْفُ عَمَّـا تَعْلَمُ ، وَأَنْتَ الْأَعَزُّ الْأَكْرَمُ.

My Lord, forgive, have mercy and pardon [us] of what You know. You are the Mightiest, the Most Generous.

The seventh cycle of the ṭawāf

رَبِّ اجْعَلْنِيْ مُقِيْمَ الصَّلَاةِ وَمِنْ ذُرِّيَّتِيْ ، رَبَّنَا وَتَقَبَّلْ دُعَاءً ، رَبَّنَا اغْفِرْ لِيْ وَلِوَالِدَيَّ وَلِلْمُؤْمِنِيْنَ يَوْمَ يَقُوْمُ الْحِسَابُ. اَللَّهُمَّ إِنِّيْ أَسْأَلُكَ إِيْمَـاناً كَامِلاً وَيَقِيْناً صَادِقاً ، وَرِزْقاً وَاسِعاً ، وَقَلْباً

خَاشِعاً ، وَلِسَاناً ذَاكِراً ، وَحَلَالاً طَيِّباً ، وَتَوْبَةً نَصُوْحاً ، وَتَوْبَةً
قَبْلَ الْـمَوْتِ، وَرَاحَةً عِنْدَ الْـمَوْتِ ، وَمَغْفِرَةً وَرَحْمَةً بَعْدَ
الْـمَوْتِ ، وَالْعَفْوَ عِنْدَ الْحِسَابِ ، وَالْفَوْزَ بِالْجَنَّةِ ،
وَالنَّجَاةَ مِنَ النَّارِ، يَا عَزِيْزُ يَا غَفَّارُ.

My Lord, make me from amongst those who establish the prayer, and from my progeny [those who do the same]. Our Lord, accept [our] supplication. Our Lord, forgive me, my parents and the believers on the day when the reckoning is established. O Allah, I ask You for perfect faith, a genuine certainty, vast sustenance, a humble heart, a remembering tongue, a pure lawful income, genuine repentance, repentance before death, ease at the time of death, forgiveness and mercy after death, pardon at the time of accountability, attainment of Paradise and salvation from the Fire, O Mighty One, O Oft-forgiver.

اَللَّهُمَّ عَلِّمْنِي مَا يَنْفَعُنِيْ ، وَانْفَعْنِي بِمَا عَلَّمْتَنِيْ ، وَزِدْنِيْ عِلْماً ،
وَأَلْحِقْنِيْ بِالصَّالِحِيْنَ ، وَاجْعَلْنِيْ مِنْ وَرَثَةِ جَنَّةِ النَّعِيْمِ ، اَللَّهُمَّ إِنَّكَ
دَعَوْتَ عِبَادَكَ إِلَى بَيْتِكَ الْحَرَامِ ، وَقَدْ جِئْتُ طَالِباً مَرْضَاتَكَ ،
وَأَنْتَ مَنَنْتَ عَلَيَّ بِذَلَكَ ، فَاغْفِرْ لِيْ وَارْحَمْنِيْ وَعَافِنِيْ وَاعْفُ
عَنِّيْ ، إِنَّكَ عَلَى كُلِّ شَيْءٍ قَدِيْرٌ.

O Allah, teach me that which will benefit me, benefit me with what You have taught me, increase my knowledge, grant me to join the righteous and make me from amongst the inheritors of the Garden of Bliss. O Allah, verily You have invited Your slaves to Your Sacred House, and I have come seeking Your pleasure, while it is You Who has favoured me with that, so forgive me, have mercy on me, grant me well-being and pardon me. Verily, You have power over everything.

رَبِّ اغْفِرْ وَارْحَمْ ، وَاعْفُ عَمَّـا تَعْلَمُ ، وَأَنْتَ الْأَعَزُّ الْأَكْرَمُ.

My Lord, forgive, have mercy and pardon [us] of what You know. You are the Mightiest, the Most Generous.

رَبَّنَا تَقَبَّلْ مِنَّا إِنَّكَ أَنْتَ السَّمِيْعُ الْعَلِيْمُ.

Our Lord, accept from us. Verily, You are the All-Hearing, the All-Knowing.

The prayer after the *ṭawāf* and its supplication

Conclude your *ṭawāf* by touching the Black Stone (or pointing to it), and then proceed to the standing place (*maqām*) of Ibrāhīm ﷺ so that it is between you and the Kaaba, or pray wherever convenient, even if it be in your room. Pray the two cycles for the [completion of] *ṭawāf* so that you may increase in your proximity to Allah, as He is the ultimate and greatest goal—and the closest a slave is to his Lord is in prostration—reading *Sūrah al-Kāfirūn* in the first cycle and *Sūrah al-Ikhlāṣ* in the second.

Upon completing the prayer, supplicate with whatever formula one desires. Amongst those supplications which have been transmitted for the occasion are the following:

اَللَّهُمَّ أَنَا عَبْدُكَ وَابْنُ عَبْدِكَ ، أَتَيْتُكَ بِذُنُوْبٍ كَبِيْرَةٍ وَ أَعْمَـالٍ
سَيِّئَةٍ ، وَهَذَا مَقامُ الْعَائِذِ بِكَ مِنَ النَّارِ، فَاغْفِرْ لِيْ إِنَّكَ
أَنْتَ الْغَفُوْرُ الرَّحِيْمُ.

O Allah, I am Your slave and the son of Your slave. I have come to You with grave sins and wrongs, and this is the place where the one taking refuge in You stands, so forgive me. Verily, You are Oft-Forgiving, the Merciful.

اَللَّهُمَّ إِنَّكَ تَعْلَمُ سِرِّيْ وَعَلَانِيَّتِيْ فَاقْبَلْ مَعْذِرَتِيْ ، وَتَعْلَمُ حَاجَتِيْ
فَأَعْطِنِيْ سُؤَالِيْ ، اَللَّهُمَّ إِنِّيْ أَسْأَلُكَ إِيْمَـاناً يُبَاشِرُ قَلْبِيْ ، وَيَقِيْناً
صَادِقاً حَتَّى أَعْلَمُ أَنَّهُ لَا يُصِيْبُنِيْ إِلَّا مَا كَتَبْتَ عَلَيَّ ،
وَرَضِّنِيْ بِمَـا قَسَمْتَ لِيْ.

O Allah, You know what I conceal and what I reveal, so accept my apology; and You know my need, so give me that which I ask. O Allah, I ask you for a faith that penetrates my heart and a genuine certainty, such that I know nothing afflicts me except what You have decreed against me, and grant me contentment with whatever You have apportioned for me.

The supplication when drinking Zamzam

It is recommended, before leaving for al-Ṣafā, to go to the Zamzam well[104] and drink from it in emulation of the

---

104 There is no access to the Zamzam well in our times and so one drinks Zamzam water from wherever available in the Mosque or the *ṭawāf* area.

Prophet's Sunnah ﷺ. One is to drink profusely (literally until one's ribs are full), and supplicate when drinking it for whatever one wishes, because it is one of the occasions where prayers are answered. It has been related in the hadith from the Prophet ﷺ, 'The water of Zamzam is for whatever [prayer] it is drunk.' Amongst the transmitted supplications when drinking Zamzam is,

اَللَّهُمَّ إِنِّيْ أَسْأَلُكَ عِلْمًا نَافِعاً ، وَرِزْقاً وَاسِعاً ، وَعَمَلاً مُتَقَبَّلاً ، وَشِفَاءً مِنْ كُلِّ دَاءٍ.

O Allah, I ask You for beneficial knowledge, vast sustenance, acceptable deeds and a cure from every ailment.

The supplication at the *Multazam*

It is recommended to hold onto the Multazam, which is the wall between the Black Stone and the door of the ennobled Kaaba, in emulation of the Prophet ﷺ; so cling unto it by placing on it your chest and right cheek, with your arms and palms stretched out vertically. Then stand in this position, humbly seeking refuge in the Lord of the House, because that is the posture of someone taking refuge and seeking safety from dangers, and this is a place wherein prayers are answered. Amongst the supplications transmitted from the scholars are,

اَللَّهُمَّ لَكَ الْحَمْدُ حَمْداً يُوَافِيْ نِعَمَكَ وَيُكَافِيءُ مَزِيْدَكَ ، أَحْمَدُكَ بِجَمِيْعِ مَحَامِدِكَ مَا عَلِمْتُ مِنْهَا وَمَا لَمْ أَعْلَمْ ، وَعَلَى كُلِّ حَالٍ.

O Allah, to You belongs the praise, a praise that is commensurate with Your blessings and reciprocative of Your additional blessings. I praise You with all of Your praises: that which I know of and that which I do not, and in every state.

اَللّٰهُمَّ صَلِّ وَسَلِّمْ عَلَى مُحَمَّدٍ وَعَلَى آلِ مُحَمَّدٍ ، اَللّٰهُمَّ أَعِذْنِيْ مِنَ الشَّيْطَانِ الرَّجِيْمِ ، وَأَعِذْنِيْ مِنْ كُلِّ سُوْءٍ، وَقَنِّعْنِيْ بِمَا رَزَقْتَنِيْ وَبَارِكْ لِيْ فِيْهِ ، اَللّٰهُمَّ اجْعَلْنِيْ مِنْ أَكْرَمِ وَفْدِكَ عَلَيْكَ ، وَأَلْزِمْنِيْ سَبِيْلَ الْإِسْتِقَامَةِ حَتَّى أَلْقَاكَ ، يَا رَبَّ الْعَالَمِيْنَ.

O Allah, send Your reverential mercy and salutations upon Muhammad and the family of Muhammad. O Allah, protect me from the accursed Satan, protect me from all evil, make me content with what You have provided me and grant me blessings therein. O Allah, make me the most honoured of Your visitors to You and enable me to adhere to the path of steadfastness until I meet You, O Lord of the Worlds.

The walk (*sa'y*) between al-Ṣafā and al-Marwah

Thereafter, it is necessary for one to walk (*sa'y*) between al-Ṣafā and al-Marwah. Therefore, emulate the exact method established from the Prophet ﷺ: he left from the door to al-Ṣafā, and as he approached al-Ṣafā, he recited,

«إِنَّ الصَّفَا وَالْمَرْوَةَ مِنْ شَعَائِرِ اللهِ فَمَنْ حَجَّ الْبَيْتَ أَوِ اعْتَمَرَ فَلَا جُنَاحَ عَلَيْهِ أَنْ يَطَّوَّفَ بِهِمَا وَمَنْ تَطَوَّعَ خَيْرًا فَإِنَّ اللهَ شَاكِرٌ عَلِيْمٌ» .أَبْدَأُ بِمَا بَدَأَ اللهُ بِهِ.

Verily al-Ṣafā and al-Marwah are from amongst the symbols of Allah; so whoever performs hajj to the House or umrah, then there is no sin upon him to go back and forth between them, and whoever voluntarily does [additional] good, then Allah is the Rewarder, the All-Knowing [Qur'an 2:158]. *I begin with what Allah began.*

So he began with al-Ṣafā, ascending it until he could see the House [Kaaba]. He then faced the qiblah and said, '*Lā ilāha illa llāh*' [There is no deity except Allah], and '*Allāhu akbar*' [Allah is the greatest].

Remember the *sa'y* of Lady Hājar, the mother of the Prophet of Allah Ismā'īl ﷺ, and realise that when a slave obeys his Master and submits to His command, he attains [Allah's] pleasure, and Allah gives him the good for which he hopes, and that by this one eradicates from oneself flaws and blemishes, thereby attaining purity (*ṣafā*).

Whenever one reaches between the two green columns on the wall of the *sa'y* area, hasten as much as possible and imagine that you are fleeing to your Lord and taking refuge in Him, in compliance with His Most High's words '*So flee to Allah*' [Qur'an 51:50].

Then, after the two columns, walk casually until you reach al-Marwah, at which point recite the verse: *Verily, al-Ṣafā and al-Marwah* ... [Qur'an 2:158], as you are ascending, and invoke Allah (by reciting the transmitted invocations) as you did on al-Ṣafā. This is a single cycle; so complete the seven cycles, beginning with the first at al-Ṣafā and ending with the last at al-Marwah. The outreach is considered one cycle and the return is another.

Again, in emulation of the Sunnah, recite thrice on al-Ṣafā and al-Marwah,

أَللهُ أَكْبَرُ ، أَللهُ أَكْبَرُ ، أَللهُ أَكْبَرُ ، وَلِلّٰـهِ الْحَمْدُ ، أَللهُ أَكْبَرُ عَلَى مَا
هَدَانَا وَالْـحَمْدُ لِلّٰـهِ عَلَى مَا أَوْلَانَا ، لَا إِلَـٰهَ إِلَّا اللهُ وَحْدَهُ لَا
شَرِيْكَ لَهُ، لَهُ الْـمُلْكُ وَلَهُ الْـحَمْدُ يُحْيِيْ وَيُمِيْتُ ، بِيَدِهِ الْخَيْرُ
وَهُوَ عَلَى كُلِّ شَيْءٍ قَدِيْرٌ، لَا إِلَهَ إِلَّا اللهُ وَحْدَهُ أَنْجزَ وَعْدَهُ ، وَنَصَرَ
عَبْدَهُ ، وَهَزَمَ الْأَحْزَابَ وَحْدَهُ ، لَا إِلَهَ إِلَّا اللهُ وَلَا نَعْبُدُ إِلَّا إِيَّاهُ
مُخْلِصِيْنَ لَهُ الدِّيْنَ وَلَو كَرِهَ الْكَافِرُوْنَ. ثَلَاثَ مَرَّاتٍ.

Allah is the greatest; Allah is the greatest; Allah is the greatest, and to Allah belongs all praise. Allah is the greatest for having guided us, and all praise belongs to Allah for what He has granted us. There is no deity except Allah, alone without a partner. To Him belongs the dominion, and to Him belongs all praise. He gives life and death; in His hand [i.e. power] is all goodness, and He has power over everything. There is no deity except Allah alone. He fulfilled His promise, supported His slave and alone defeated the confederates. There is no deity except Allah, and we worship Him alone, sincerely adhering to His religion, even if the disbelievers are averse to [it].

اَللَّهُمَّ إِنَّكَ قُلْتَ : «**أُدْعُوْنِيْ أَسْتَجِبْ لَكُمْ**،» وَإِنَّكَ لَا تُخْلِفُ
الْـمِيْعَادَ ، وَإِنِّيْ أَسَأَلُكَ كَمَـا هَدَيْتَنِيْ لِلْإِسْلَامِ أَلَّا تَنْزِعَهُ مِنِّيْ
حَتَّى تَتَوَفَّانِيْ وَأَنَا مُسْلِمٌ.

O Allah, verily You have said, 'Supplicate to me, and I shall answer you,' and verily You do not break Your promise, and so I ask You that just as You have guided me to Islam, do not divest me of it; [so please]take my life as a Muslim!

It is a sunnah for one to prolong one's standing on al-Ṣafā and al-Marwah, invoking blessings upon the Prophet ﷺ, supplicating and reciting in each cycle as you descend from al-Ṣafā,

اَللَّهُمَّ اسْتَعْمِلْنِي بِسُّنَةِ نَبِيِّكَ ، وَتَوَفَّنِيْ عَلَى مِلَّتِهِ ، وَأَعِذْنِيْ مِنْ مُضِلَّاتِ الْفِتَنِ بِرَحْمَتِكَ ، يَا أَرْحَمَ الرَّاحِمِيْنَ.

O Allah, utilise me in accordance with the Sunnah of Your Prophet, grant me to die adhering to his religion; and out of your mercy, protect me from misguiding tribulations, O Most Merciful of the Merciful.

And recite during the *saʿy* as you are between the two green columns,

رَبِّ اغْفِرْ وَارْحَمْ وَتَجَاوَزْ عَمَّـا تَعْلَمُ إِنَّكَ أَنْتَ الْأَعَزُّ الْأَكْرَمُ.

My Lord, forgive, have mercy and pardon [us] of what You know. Verily, You are the Mightiest, the Most Generous.

رَبَّنَا آتِنَا فِي الدُّنْيَا حَسَنَةً وَفِي الْآخِرَةِ حَسَنَةً وَقِنَا عَذَابَ النَّارِ.

O our Lord, give us good in this world and good in the next world, and guard us from the torment of the Fire.

Strive in your supplication with whatever Allah inspires you, and invoke blessings upon the Prophet ﷺ, and read the Qur'an with a low-pitched voice.

The supplications during the cycles of the *sa'y*

There follows numerous supplications that one can recite, together with the previous supplications and those read in *ṭawāf*, in addition to whatever Allah inspires in one of supplications, invocations and recitation of the Qur'an.

The first cycle of the sa'y

اَللَّهُمَّ اعْصِمْنِيْ بِدِيْنِكَ وَطَوَاعِيَّتِكَ وَطَاعَةِ رَسُوْلِكَ ، وَجَنِّبْنِيْ حُدُوْدَكَ ، اَللَّهُمَّ اجْعَلْنِيْ أُحِبُّكَ ، وَأُحِبُّ مَلَائِكَتَكَ وَأَنْبِيَاءَكَ وَرُسُلَكَ وَأُحِبُّ عِبَادَكَ الصَّالِحِيْنَ ، اَللَّهُمَّ يَسِّرْ لِيَ الْيُسْرَى، وَجَنِّبْنِيَ الْعُسْرَى ، وَاغْفِرْ لِيْ فِي الْآخِرَةِ وَالْأُوْلَى ، وَاجْعَلْنِيْ مِنْ أَئِمَّةِ الْمُتَّقِيْنَ ، اَللَّهُمَّ نَجِّنَا مِنَ النَّارِ مَعَ عِبَادِكَ الصَّالِحِيْنَ، مَعَ الَّذِيْنَ أَنْعَمَ اللهُ عَلَيْهِمْ مِنَ النَّبِيِّيْنَ وَالصِّدِّيْقِيْنَ وَالشُّهَدَاءِ وَالصَّالِحِيْنَ ، وَحَسُنَ أُوْلَئِكَ رَفِيْقاً.

O Allah, protect me by virtue of your religion and my submission to You and obedience to Your Messenger, and keep me remote from Your limits [i.e. prohibitions]. O Allah, make me love You, love Your angels, love Your prophets and messengers and love Your righteous slaves. O Allah, facilitate for me Paradise, keep me away from Hellfire [literally hardship], forgive me in the latter and the former, and make me from amongst the leaders of the God-conscious. O Allah, save me from the Fire, together with Your righteous slaves, together with those whom You have blessed of the prophets, the truly veracious [ṣiddīqīn], the martyrs and the righteous, and what beautiful companions those are!

لَا إِلَـٰهَ إِلَّا اللهُ حَقّاً حَقّاً ، لَا إِلَـٰهَ إِلَّا اللهُ تَعَبُّداً وَرِقّاً ، لَا إِلَـٰهَ إِلَّا اللهُ
وَلَا نَعْبُدُ إِلَّا إِيَّاهُ مُخْلِصِيْنَ لَهُ الدِّيْنَ ، وَلَو كَرِهَ الْكَافِرُوْنَ ، وَلَا حَوْلَ
وَلَا قُوَّةَ إِلَّا بِاللهِ الْعَلِيِّ الْعَظِيْمِ. وَحَسْبُنَا اللهُ وَنِعْمَ الْوَكِيْلِ.

There is truly, truly, no deity except Allah; there is no deity worthy of worship and [our] slavehood except Allah. There is no deity except Allah, and we do not worship other than Him, adhering to the religion exclusively for Him, even if the disbelievers are averse. There is no strategy or power except through Allah, the Exalted, the Great, and Allah is sufficient for us, and what a beautiful guardian He is!

The second cycle of the **saʿy**

اَللَّهُمَّ اجْعَلْنِيْ مِنْ أَئِمَّةِ الْـمُتَّقِيْنَ ، وَمِنْ وَرَثَةِ جَنَّةِ النَّعِيْمِ ،
اَللَّهُمَّ اغْفِرْ لِيْ خَطِيْئَتِيْ يَوْمَ الدِّيْنِ ، اَللَّهُمَّ لَا تُقَدِّمْنِيْ لِتَعْذِيْبٍ ،
وَلَا تُؤَخِّرْنِيْ لِشَتَّى الْفِتَنِ ، اَللَّهُمَّ أَحْيِنِيْ عَلَى سُنَّةِ نَبِيِّكَ
وَاسْتَعْمِلْنِيْ بِهَا ، وَتَوَفَّنِيْ عَلَى مِلَّتِهِ وَأَعِذْنِيْ مِنْ شَرِّ مُضِلَّاتِ
الْفِتَنِ ، اَللَّهُمَّ إِنِّيْ أَعُوْذُ بِكَ مِنَ الْـمَأْثَمِ وَالْـمَغْرَمِ.

O Allah, make me from amongst the leaders of the God-conscious and from amongst the inheritors of the Garden of Bliss. O Allah, forgive me my faults on the Day of Reckoning. O Allah, do not bring me forth to be punished, and do not leave me behind subject to various tribulations. O Allah, make my life accord with the Sunnah of Your Prophet and employ me in accordance with it, grant me to die adhering to his religion, and protect me from the evil of misguiding tribulations. O Allah, I take refuge in You from sins and debts.

لَا إِلَـٰهَ إِلَّا اللهُ الْوَاحِدُ الْأَحَدُ ، لَا إِلَـٰهَ إِلَّا اللهُ الْفَرْدُ الصَّمَدُ ، اَلَّذِيْ لَمْ يَتَّخِذْ صَاحِبَةً وَلَا وَلَداً، وَلَمْ يَكُنْ لَهُ شَرِيْكٌ فِي الْـمُلْكِ ، وَلَمْ يَكُنْ لَهُ وَلِيٌّ مِنَ الذُّلِّ وَكَبِّرْهُ تَكْبِيْراً.

There is no deity except Allah, the One, the Unique. There is no deity except Allah, the Lone, the Independent, the One who has neither taken a spouse, nor a child, and He has no partner in His dominion, nor an ally out of weakness. And invoke that He is the Greatest.

The third cycle of the sa'y

اَللَّهُمَّ يَا مُقَلِّبَ الْقُلُوْبِ ، ثَبِّتْ قَلْبِيْ عَلَى دِيْنِكَ ، اَللَّهُمَّ إِنِّيْ أَسْأَلُكَ مُوْجِبَاتِ رَحْمَتِكَ ، وَعَزَائِمَ مَغْفِرَتِكَ ، وَ الْغَنِيْمَةَ مِنْ كُلِّ بِرٍّ ، وَالسَّلَامَةَ مِنْ كُلِّ إِثْمٍ ، وَالْفَوْزَ بِالْجَنَّةِ ، وَالنَّجَاةَ مِنَ النَّارِ.

O Allah, O Turner of Hearts, make my heart resolute upon Your religion. O Allah, I ask You for those things that necessitate Your mercy, deeds that ensure Your forgiveness, effortless attainment of every good, safety from every sin, attainment of Paradise and salvation from the Fire.

اَللَّهُمَّ إِنِّيْ أَسْأَلُكَ الْهُدَى وَالتُّقَى وَالْعَفَافَ وَالْغِنَى ، اَللَّهُمَّ أَعِنِّيْ
عَلَى ذِكْرِكَ وَشُكْرِكَ وَحُسْنِ عِبَادَتِكَ.

O Allah, I ask You for guidance, piety, integrity and affluence [contentment]. O Allah, help me to remember You, thank You and worship You well.

رَبِّ زِدْنِيْ عِلْماً ، وَلَا تُزِغْ قَلْبِيْ بَعْدَ إِذْ هَدَيْتَنِيْ ،
وَهَبْ لِيْ مِنْ لَدُنْكَ رَحْمَةً إِنَّكَ أَنْتَ الْوَهَّابُ.

My Lord, increase my knowledge, and do not deviate my heart after having guided me, and grant me from Yourself a mercy. Verily, You are the Benevolent.

اَللَّهُمَّ عَافِنِيْ فِيْ سَمْعِيْ ، وَعَافِنِيْ فِيْ بَصَرِيْ ، لَا إِلَهَ إِلَّا أَنْتَ ،
سُبْحَانَكَ إِنِّيْ كُنْتُ مِنَ الظَّالِمِيْنَ ، ظَلَمْتُ نَفْسِيْ فَاغْفِرْ لِيْ
فَإِنَّهُ لَا يَغْفِرُ الذُّنُوْبَ إِلَّا أَنْتَ.

O Allah, protect my hearing and sight. There is no deity except You. Glory be to You. Verily, I have been from the oppressors; I have oppressed myself, so forgive me, for verily no one forgives sins except You.

اَللَّهُمَّ إِنِّيْ أَعُوْذُ بِكَ مِنَ الْكُفْرِ وَالْفَقْرِ ، اَللَّهُمَّ إِنِّي أَعُوْذُ بِرِضَاكَ
مِنْ سَخَطِك ، وَأَعُوْذُ بِمُعَافَاتِكَ مِنْ عُقُوْبَتِكَ، وَأَعُوْذُ بِكَ
مِنْكَ ، لَا أُحْصِيْ ثَنَاءً عَلَيْكَ أَنْتَ كَمَا أَثْنَيْتَ عَلَى نَفْسِكَ ،
فَلَكَ الْحَمْدُ حَتَّى تَرْضَى.

O Allah, I take refuge in You from disbelief and poverty. O Allah, I take refuge in Your pleasure from Your displeasure and in Your protection from Your punishment, and I take refuge in You from You. I am unable to exhaust praise for You as You have praised Yourself; so all praise belongs to You until You are pleased.

***The fourth cycle of the* sa'y**

اَللَّهُمَّ إِنِّيْ أَسْأَلُكَ مِنَ الْخَيْرِ كُلِّهِ مَا عَلِمْتُ مِنْهُ وَمَا لَمْ أَعْلَمْ ،
وَأَعُوْذُ بِكَ مِنَ الشَّرِّ كُلِّهِ مَا عَلِمْتُ مِنْهُ وَمَا لَمْ أَعْلَمْ ، اَللَّهُمَّ إِنِّيْ
أَسْأَلُكَ الْجَنَّةَ وَمَا قَرَّبَ إِلَيْهَا مِنْ قَوْلٍ أَوْ عَمَلٍ، وَأَعُوْذُ بِكَ مِنَ
النَّارِ وَمَا قَرَّبَ إِلَيْهَا مِنْ قَوْلٍ أَوْ عَمَلٍ.

O Allah, I ask You for all goodness: that which I know of and that which I do not, and I take refuge in You from all evil: that which I know of and that which I do not. O Allah, I ask You for Paradise and those words and deeds that bring one close to it, and I take refuge in You from the Fire and those words and deeds that bring one close to it.

حَسْبِيَ اللهُ وَكَفَى ، سَمِعَ اللهُ لِـمَنْ دَعَا لَيْسَ وَرَاءَ اللهِ مُنْتَهَى.

Allah is enough for me and sufficient. Allah hears the one who supplicates [Him]. There is no goal beyond Allah.

اَللَّهُمَّ إِنِّيْ أَسْأَلُكَ مِنْ خَيْرِ مَا تَعْلَمُ ، وَأَعُوْذُ بِكَ مِنْ شَرِّ مَا تَعْلَمُ، وَأَسْتَغْفِرُكَ مِنْ كُلِّ مَا تَعْلَمُ ، إِنَّكَ أَنْتَ عَلَّامُ الْغُيُوْبِ ، لَا إِلَهَ إِلَّا اللهُ الْـمَلِكُ الْحَقُّ الْـمُبِيْنُ ، مُحَمَّدٌ رَسُوْلُ اللهِ الصَّادِقُ الْوَعْدِ الْأَمِيْنُ، اَللَّهُمّ إِنِّيْ أَعُوْذُ بِكَ مِنْ وَسَاوِسِ الصَّدْرِ، وَمِنْ شَتَاتِ الْأَمْرِ ، وَمِنْ فِتْنَةِ الْقَبْرِ ، اَللَّهُمَّ إِنِّيْ أَعُوْذُ بِكَ مِنْ شَرِّ مَا يَلِجُ فِي اللَّيْلِ وَشَرِّ مَا يَلِجُ فِي النَّهَارِ، وَمِنْ شَرِّ مَا تَهُبُّ بِهِ الرِّيَاحُ ، يَا أَرْحَمَ الرَّاحِمِيْنَ.

O Allah, I ask You for the good that You know of, and I take refuge in You from the evil that You know of, and I seek Your forgiveness for everything that You know of. Verily, You are All-Knowing of the Unseen. There is no deity except Allah, the Sovereign, the Manifest Truth, and Muhammad is the Messenger of Allah, the one true to his promise, the trustworthy. O Allah, I take refuge in You from the evil of [satanic] whisperings within my heart, [from] disarray and tribulation in the grave. O Allah, verily I take refuge in You from the evil of what enters the night, the evil of what enters the day and the evil of what the winds blow, O Most Merciful of the Merciful.

سُبْحَانَكَ مَا عَبَدْنَاكَ حَقَّ عِبَادَتِكَ ، سُبْحَانَكَ
مَا ذَكَرْنَاكَ حَقَّ ذِكْرِكَ يَا اللهُ.

Glory be to You; we have not worshipped You as You deserve to be worshipped. Glory be to You; we have not remembered You as You deserve to be remembered, O Allah.

The fifth cycle of the saʿy

اَللَّهُمَّ إِنِّيْ أَعُوْذُ بِكَ مِنَ الْهَمِّ وَالْحَزَنِ ، وَأَعُوْذُ بِكَ مِنَ الْعَجْزِ
وَالْكَسَلِ ، وَأَعُوْذُ بِكَ مِنَ الْجُبْنِ وَالْبُخْلِ ، وَأَعُوْذُ بِكَ
مِنْ غَلَبَةِ الدَّيْنِ وَقَهْرِ الرِّجَالِ.

O Allah, I take refuge in You from anxiety and distress, debilitation and laziness, cowardice and miserliness, and from being over burdened by debt and subjugated by men.

يَا حَيُّ يَا قَيُّوْمُ بِرَحْمَتِكَ أَسْتَغِيْثُ ، أَعِذْنِيْ مِنْ شَرِّ نَفْسِيْ
وَمِنْ شَرِّ الشَّيْطَانِ وَشِرْكِهِ ، وَمِنْ شَرِّ كُلِّ دَابَّةٍ أَنْتَ آخِذٌ
بِنَاصِيَتِهَا، إِنَّ رَبِّيْ عَلَى صِرَاطٍ مُسْتَقِيْمٍ.

O Living, O Self-Sufficient Sustainer, by your mercy I seek assistance. Protect me from the evil of myself, from the evil of Satan and his [tempting us to commit] idolatry, and from the evil of every beast whose forelock is in Your grasp. Verily, my Lord is on a straight path [of truth and justice].

سُبْحَانَكَ مَا شَكَرْنَاكَ حَقَّ شُكْرِكَ ، سُبْحَانَكَ مَا أَعْظَمَ شَأْنَكَ.

Glory be to You; we have not shown You gratitude as You deserve. Glory be to You; how tremendous is Your rank!

اَللَّهُمَّ اهْدِنِيْ بِالْهُدَى وَنَقِّنِيْ بِالتَّقْوَى وَاغْفِرْ لِيْ فِي الْآخِرَةِ وَالْأُوْلَى، اَللَّهُمَّ ابْسُطْ عَلَيْنَا مِنْ بَرَكَاتِك وَرَحْمَتِكَ ، اَللَّهُمَّ أَفِضْ عَلَيْنَا مِنْ فَضْلِكَ وَرِزْقِكَ ، اَللَّهُمَّ إِنِّيْ أَسْأَلُكَ النَّعِيْمَ الْـمُقِيْمَ الَّذِيْ لَا يَحُوْلُ وَلَا يَزوْلُ أَبَداً فِيْ أَعْلَى دَرَجِ الْجَنَّةِ جَنَّةِ الْخُلْدِ ، رَبِّ اشْرَحْ لِيْ صَدْرِيْ وَيَسِّرْ لِيْ أَمْرِيْ.

O Allah, guide me with [Your] guidance, purify me with piety and forgive me in the latter and the former [life]. O Allah, spread forth for us from Your blessings and mercy. O Allah, shower on us from Your bounty and sustenance. O Allah, I ask You for perpetual bliss that never fluctuates, nor disappears, in the most elevated degree of Paradise: the Paradise of Eternity. My Lord, open my heart and facilitate for me my affair.

The sixth cycle of the saʿy

اَللَّهُمَّ إِنِّيْ أَسْأَلُكَ حُبَّكَ وَحُبَّ نَبِيِّكَ مُحَمَّدٍ ﷺ وَأَنْ تَجْعَلَ حُبَّكَ وَحُبَّ نَبِيِّكَ أَحَبَّ إِلَيَّ مِنْ نَفْسِيْ وَأَهْلِيْ وَمِنَ الدُّنْيَا كُلِّهَا وَمِنَ الْـمَـاءِ الْبَارِدِ عَلَى الظَّمَأِ.

O Allah, I ask You for Your love and the love of Your Prophet Muhammad ﷺ, and that you make Your love and the love of Your Prophet more beloved to me than myself, my family, this entire world and cold water when thirsty.

اَللَّهُمَّ إِنِّيْ أَسْأَلُكَ مُرَافَقَةَ نَبِيِّكَ فِيْ أَعْلَى دَرَجِ الْجَنَّةِ جَنَّةِ الْخُلْدِ.

O Allah, I ask You for the company of Your Prophet in the highest degree of Paradise: the Paradise of Eternity.

اَللَّهُمَّ بِنُوْرِكَ اهْتَدَيْنَا ، وَبِفَضْلِكَ اسْتَغْنَيْنَا ، وَفِيْ كَنَفِكَ وَإِنْعَامِكَ وَعَطَائِكَ وَإِحْسَانِكَ وَإِكْرَامِكَ أَصْبَحْنَا وَأَمْسَيْنَا.

O Allah, by Your light, we have been guided; by Your Grace, made self-sufficient, and in Your care, blessing, giving, kindness and generosity, we enter the morning and evening.

أَنْتَ الْأَوَّلُ فَلَيْسَ قَبْلَكَ شَيْءٌ ، وَأَنْتَ الْآخِرُ فَلَيْسَ بَعْدَكَ شَيْءٌ ، وَأَنْتَ الظَّاهِرُ فَلَيْسَ فَوْقَكَ شَيْءٌ ، وَأَنْتَ الْبَاطِنُ فَلَيْسَ دُوْنَكَ شَيْءٌ.

You are the first; so there is nothing before You. You are the last; so there is nothing after You. You are the manifest; so there is nothing above You. You are the hidden; so there is nothing beneath You.

اَللَّهُمَّ إِنِّيْ أَعُوْذُ بِكَ مِنَ الْفَلَسِ وَالْكَسَلِ ، وَعَذَابِ الْقَبْرِ،
وَ أَعُوْذُ بِكَ مِنْ شَرِّ فِتْنَةِ الْغِنَى وَمِنْ شَرِّ فِتْنَةِ الْفَقْرِ، وَ مِنْ شَرِّ
فِتْنَةِ الْـمَسِيْحِ الدَّجَّالِ، وَأَسْأَلُكَ الْفَوْزَ بِالْجَنَّةِ وَالنَّجَاةَ
مِنَ النَّارِ، يَا عَزِيْزُ يَا غَفَّارَ، يَا أَرْحَمَ الرَّاحِمِيْنَ.

O Allah, I take refuge in You from bankruptcy, lethargy and the torment in the grave. I take refuge in You from the evil in the tribulation of affluence, the evil in the tribulation of poverty and the evil in the tribulation of the False Messiah. And I ask You for the attainment of Paradise and salvation from the Fire, O Mighty One, O Oft-Forgiver, O Most Merciful of the Merciful.

The seventh cycle of the saʿy

اَللَّهُمَّ إِنِّيْ أَسْأَلُكَ خَيْرَ مَا سَأَلَكَ عِبَادُكَ الصَّالِحُوْنَ ،
وَ أَعُوْذُ بِكَ مِنْ شَرِّ مَا اسْتَعَاذَكَ عِبَادُكَ الصَالِحُوْنَ ، اَللَّهُمَّ
مَا أَعْطَيْتَ أَحداً سَعَى بِهٰـذَا الْـمَكَانِ مِنْ رُتْبَةٍ أَوْ ثَوَابٍ سَأَلْتُكَ
إِيَّاهُ أَوْ قَصُرَ عَنْـهُ دُعَائِي فَأَعْطِنِيْ إِيَّـاهُ وَامْنَحْنِيْ إِيَّـاهُ مِنْ
فَضْلِكَ وَكَـرَمِكَ وَإِحْسَانِكَ، يَا قَدِيْمَ الْإِحْسَانِ ،
يَا كَثِيْرَ الْخَيْرَاتِ ، يَا دَائِمَ الْمَعْرُوْفِ.

O Allah, I ask You for the best of what Your righteous slaves have asked You, and I take refuge in You from the worst of what Your righteous slaves have sought refuge in You. O Allah, whatever rank or reward You have given to whoever has performed the saʿy in this place, then I ask You for it, or [of which] my supplication fell short, then give me it, and grant me it out of Your grace, generosity and kindness, O Pre-Eternally kind, O Abundant in Good, O Eternally Generous.

اَللَّهُمَّ اخْتِمْ بِالْخَيْرَاتِ الْبَاقِيَاتِ الصَّالِحَاتِ آجَالَنَا وَأَعْمَالَنَا حَتَّى نَلْقَاكَ وَأَنْتَ رَاضٍ عَنَّا.

O Allah, conclude our lives and actions with continuous righteous deeds, so that we meet You [with You] satisfied with us.

اَللَّهُمَّ حَقِّقْ بِفَضْلِكَ آمَالَنَا ، وَسَهِّلْ لِبُلُوْغِ رِضَاكَ سُبُلَنَا ، وَحَسِّنْ فِيْ جَمِيْعِ الْأَحْوَالِ أَعْمَالَنَا ، يَا مُنْقِذَ الْغَرْقَى ، يَا مُنْجِيَ الْهَلْكَى ، يَا شَاهِدَ كُلِّ نَجْوَى ، يَا مُنْتَهَى كُلِّ شَكْوَى ، يَا قَدِيْمَ الْإِحْسَانِ ، يَا دَائِمَ الْمَعْرُوْفِ.

O Allah, out of Your Grace fulfil our hopes, facilitate our paths in attaining Your pleasure, and beautify our deeds in all conditions, O Rescuer of the Drowning, O Saviour of the Perishing, O Witness of every private conversation, O Ultimate [to whom people resort] for every complaint, O Pre-eternally Kind, O Eternally Generous.

اَللَّهُمَّ إِنِّيْ عَائِذٌ بِكَ مِنْ شَرِّ مَا أَعْطَيْتَنَا وَ مِنْ شَرِّ مَا مَنَعْتَنَا ، وَمِنْ شَرِّ مَا عَمِلْنَا وَشَرِّ مَا لَمْ نَعْمَلْ ، اَللَّهُمَّ يَسِّرْ لَنَا أَمْرَنَا كُلَّهُ ، وَأَجِرْنَا مِنْ خِزْيِ الدُّنْيَا وَعَذَابِ الْآخِرَةِ.

O Allah, I take refuge in You from the evil in what You have given us, from the evil of what You have withheld from us, from the evil of what we have done and from the evil of what we have not done. O Allah, facilitate for us every affair of ours, and protect us from humiliation in this world and punishment in the next.

رَبَّنَا تَقَبَّلْ مِنَّا إِنَّكَ أَنْتَ السَّمِيْعُ الْعَلِيْمُ ، وَاغْفِرْ لَنَا إِنَّكَ أَنْتَ الْغَفُوْرُ الرَّحِيْمُ.

Our Lord, accept from us; verily, You are the All-Hearing, the All-Knowing, and forgive us; verily, You are the All-Forgiving, the Compassionate.

Release from the state of *iḥrām* for a *mutamatti*ʿ pilgrim and the one performing umrah only

Upon completing the *saʿy*, shave the head with a blade or shorten one's hair [to the required level]. The minimum amount one cuts is the length of the end joint of a finger [approximately an inch long]. A woman, however, only cuts her hair [sufficiently] short and does not shave it.

By shaving or shortening the hair the umrah is complete, and all the prohibitions whilst in *iḥrām* once again become lawful. This release is for whoever observes the *iḥrām* for umrah, whether he intends to observe the *iḥrām* thereafter for hajj, in which case he is a *mutamatti*ʿ, or intends to confine himself to performing umrah.

The *mufrid* and the *qārin*

However, if one is a *mufrid*, intending hajj only, do not shave the head nor shorten the hair [to the required amount], as one is not to release oneself from *iḥrām*; rather, one is to remain in the state of *iḥrām*. Consequently, one's *ṭawāf* is the *Ṭawāf of* Arrival (*Ṭawāf al-Qudūm*), and the *sa'y* one performs counts for one as the necessary *sa'y* for hajj.

However, if one is a *qārin*, intending hajj and umrah (simultaneously), do not shave the head or release oneself from *iḥrām*. In this case, one's *ṭawāf* and *sa'y* accounts for umrah. It is, furthermore, incumbent on one to perform the *Ṭawāf* of Arrival and *sa'y* for hajj after it if one wishes to perform the *sa'y* for hajj early,[105] which is better; however, if one wishes, one can postpone it till after the *Ṭawāf* of the Visit (*Ṭawāf al-Ziyārah*) [the obligatory *ṭawāf*] on the Day of Sacrifice.

Staying in Mecca

Thereafter, remain in Mecca, profusely performing acts of worship, obedience and charity therein, because a good deed is multiplied there [in reward] due to what has been related from the Prophet ﷺ, 'A prayer in this mosque of mine is better than a thousand prayers in any other mosque, except for the Sacred Mosque [in Mecca], and a prayer in the Sacred Mosque is better than hundred prayers in this [mosque].'

---

105 The other schools consider the first *ṭawāf* and *sa'y* as sufficient, as is the case for someone performing hajj only (*mufrid*). However, it is more precautionary to adopt the opinion of the Ḥanafis in this matter.

Circumambulate the House whenever one can, because the Prophet ﷺ said, 'The *ṭawāf* is a prayer,' and prayer is the best act of worship legislated, and so likewise is the *ṭawāf*. Moreover, pray in the *Ḥijr* of Ismāʿīl, as it is part of the Kaaba. This *Ḥijr* is the *Ḥaṭim,* and praying therein is similar to praying in the Kaaba, and it is amongst the places wherein one's prayers are answered; so supplicate with whatever Allah inspires in one. The following is one of the transmitted prayers for when one is in the *Ḥijr*,

يَا رَبِّ أَتَيْتُكَ مِنْ شُقَّةٍ بَعِيْدَةٍ مُؤَمِّلاً مَعْرُوْفَكَ ، فَأَنِلْنِيْ
مَعْرُوْفاً مِنْ مَعْرُوْفِكَ تُغْنِيْنِيْ بِهِ عَنْ مَعْرُوْفِ مَنْ سِوَاكَ ،
يَا مَعْرُوْفاً بِالْمَعْرُوْفِ.

O my Lord, I have come to You from a remote land,
hoping for Your generosity and gifts, so grant me one
of Your gifts that will spare me of anyone else's gift,
O the One known for generosity.

Entering the revered Kaaba

It is recommended to enter the revered House as long as one does not, due to congestion, annoy anyone, which is rarely possible. It is necessary that one adhere to the proper etiquette, externally and internally, and observe the grandeur of the House and its sanctity. Pray therein two cycles in whichever direction, and it is recommended after the prayer for whoever has prayed in it to place his cheek on the wall of the Kaaba and to seek forgiveness from Allah Most High and praise Him.Then go to the [four] corners [of the Kaaba] and praise Allah and invoke the formula

'*Lā ilāha illa llāh*' [There is no deity except Allah] and the formula '*Subḥānallāh*' [Glory be to Allah], and ask Allah Most High for whatever one wants, as all of the above actions have been related from the Prophet ﷺ.

When one sits in the Sacred Mosque, continuously gaze at the Ancient House, out of yearning for it, seeking help from its blessings (*barakāt*) and veneration for it, since gazing at it is an act of worship by which mercies descend.[106]

On the seventh day of Dhū al-Ḥijjah, listen to the sermon of the imam in which he admonishes the congregation and teaches them the rules of *iḥrām* and the actions required of them; and they are the rituals of the second stage: the hajj rituals.

How to perform hajj and its supplications

The most important rituals during hajj are the following:

1. the *iḥrām*;
2. standing in ʿArafah;
3. standing in al-Muzdalifah;
4. stoning [the ʿAqabah site] on the Day of Eid;
5. the sacrifice;
6. shaving one's head [or shortening the hair];
7. the *Ṭawāf* of the Visit (*Ṭawāf al-Ziyārah*);
8. the *saʿy*;
9. stoning the [three] sites on the Days of *Tashrīq*;
10. and the Farewell *Ṭawāf* (*Ṭawāf al-Wadāʿ*).

---

106 [T] It has been related from the Prophet ﷺ that he said, 'Everyday, Allah sends down upon the pilgrims to His Inviolable House one hundred and twenty portions of mercy: sixty for those performing *ṭawāf*, forty for those praying and twenty for those gazing (i.e. at the Kaaba).' Sirāj al-Dīn, ʿAbd-Allāh. *Manāsik al-ḥajj*, 38.

The hajj rituals are performed over six days, and these are:

1. eighth Dhū al-Ḥijjah: it is called the day of *Tarwiyah* [the Day of Quenching Thirst] because the early pilgrims used to give their camels water in preparation for hajj, and it is on this day that the *mutamatti*ʿ pilgrim initiates his *iḥrām* and all pilgrims proceed towards Minā;
2. ninth Dhū al-Ḥijjah: on this day is the standing in ʿArafah, followed by [spending the night in] al-Muzdalifah;
3. tenth Dhū al-Ḥijjah: the Day of the Eid of Sacrifice. On this day, one observes the following rituals:

    a. stoning the site of ʿAqabah;
    b. the sacrifice;
    c. shaving one's head;
    d. the *Ṭawāf* of the Visit (*Ṭawāf al-Ziyārah*);
    e. and the *sa*ʿ*y* [if not performed earlier];

4. eleventh Dhū al-Ḥijjah: it is the first day of *Tashrīq*, and during it all the sites are stoned;
5. twelfth Dhū al-Ḥijjah: which is the second day of *Tashrīq*, and it is called the Day of the First Departure (*Yawm al-Nafr al-Awwal*) because during it the three sites are stoned, followed by the pilgrims hastily departing for Mecca;
6. and thirteenth Dhū al-Ḥijjah: the third day of *Tashrīq*, also called the Day of the Second Departure (*Yawm al-Nafr al-Thānī*), and on this day the three sites are stoned, followed by the pilgrims leaving for Mecca. They then perform the Farewell *Ṭawāf* (*Ṭawāf al-Wadā*ʿ).

The tenth, eleventh and twelfth days of Dhū al-Ḥijjah are called the Days of Sacrifice, and the eleventh day and those thereafter are called the Days of *Tashrīq*.

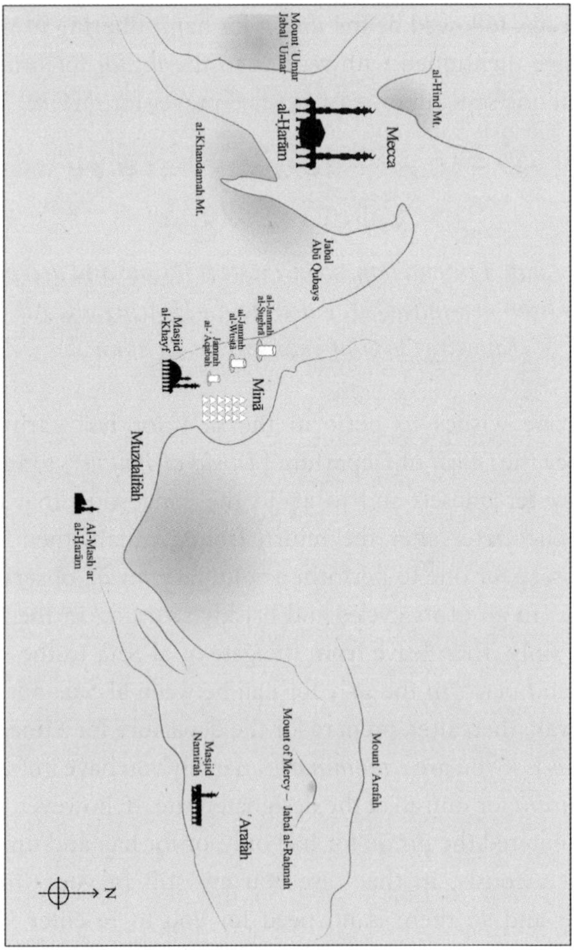

Figure 3: The holy places and sites (*al-Mashāʿir*) wherein the hajj rites are performed.

The daily rites of hajj

The Day of Tarwiyah

When the Day of *Tarwiyah* arrives, perform the *fajr* prayer in Mecca, followed by the *iḥrām* for hajj, adhering to what we have mentioned with respect to the *iḥrām* for umrah, except one says after the two cycled prayer for *iḥrām*,

اَللَّهُمَّ إِنِّيْ أُرِيْدُ الْحَجَّ فَيَسِّرْهُ لِيْ وَتَقَبَّلْهُ مِنِّيْ ، إِنَّكَ أَنْتَ السَّمِيْعُ الْعَلِيْمُ . لَبَّيْكَ اللَّهُمَّ ...

O Allah, I intend hajj, so facilitate it for me and accept it from me. Indeed, You are the All-Hearing, the All-Knowing. Ever at your service, O Allah ...

If one wishes to perform the *saʿy* for hajj early on (before the *Ṭawāf* of Departure [*Ṭawāf al-Ifāḍah*]) to make it easy for oneself and to avoid the congestion that one may encounter after the return from ʿArafah, then it is necessary for one to perform a voluntary *ṭawāf*, observing *iḍṭibāʿ* in all of its cycles and briskly strutting in the first three only. Then leave from the gate of al-Ṣafā to the *saʿy* area and perform the *saʿy* for hajj between al-Ṣafā and al-Marwah; thereafter, prepare for the departure for Minā.

This is if you are a *mutamattiʿ*, namely you have initiated the *iḥrām* for umrah at the designated site. If, however, you have entered the *iḥrām* for hajj only, or for hajj and umrah simultaneously, in that case you are still in your initial *iḥrām* and so there is no need for you to re-enter your *iḥrām*; you are only required to proceed to Minā.

It is a sunnah for one to set off for Minā after sunrise and remain there until after sunrise on the Day of ʿArafah, performing therein the five prayers: *ẓuhr*, *ʿaṣr*, *maghrib*, *ʿishā'* and *fajr*, in emulation of the Prophet ﷺ.

When heading towards Minā, recite this supplication:

اَللَّهُمَّ إِيَّاكَ أَرْجُوْ ، وَلَكَ أَدْعُوْ ، فَبَلِّغْنِيْ صَالِحَ أَمَلِيْ ، وَاغْفِرْ لِيْ ذُنُوْبِيْ ، وَامْنُنْ عَلَيَّ بِمَا مَنَنْتَ بِهِ عَلَى أَهْلِ طَاعَتِكَ ، إِنَّكَ عَلَى كُلِّ شَيْءٍ قَدِيْرٌ.

O Allah, I have placed my hopes in You, and to You I supplicate; so allow me to attain my righteous hopes, forgive me my sins and favour me with whatever You have favoured Your obedient ones. Verily, You have power over everything.

The wisdom in staying overnight in Minā is to prepare for the standing in ʿArafah and to attain one's wishes (*munā*); therefore, wish from Allah, beseeching Him for a state that is better, pure from sins and facilitated in acquiring more good deeds than one's former state. Moreover, profusely recite the *talbiyah*, Qur'an and all other invocations, supplications and the following words:

رَبَّنَا آتِنَا فِي الدُّنْيَا حَسَنَةً وَفِي الْآخِرَةِ حَسَنَةً وَقِنَا عَذَابَ النَّارِ.

Our Lord, give us good in this world and good in the next world, and protect us from the torment of the Fire.

The Day of ʿArafah

There are two matters which are necessary for you to do on this great day:[107]

1. the standing in ʿArafah;
2. and then followed by the standing in al-Muzdalifah.

PROCEEDING TOWARDS ʿARAFAH

When one has performed the *fajr* prayer on the Day of ʿArafah in Minā, it is a sunnah for one to stay there until sunrise, deposit one's luggage in Minā and make arrangements for one's needs, such as food and the like. Travel light to ʿArafah so that one's heart is not pre-occupied with anything but complete devotion to the Lord of Creation. When the sun rises, set off for ʿArafah to perform the greatest integral of hajj, inwardly calm and outwardly dignified in one's works and conduct, chanting the *talbiyah*, the invocation that '*Lā ilāha illa llāh*' [There is no deity except Allah] and '*Allāhu akbar*' [Allah is the greatest], and supplicating and remembering Allah Most High, all the while profusely chanting the *talbiyah*.

It is recommended that one recite the following when proceeding towards ʿArafah,

---

107 [T] The Prophet ﷺ said about the Day of ʿArafah, 'This is a day wherein the one who controls his hearing, sight and tongue will be forgiven.' [Narrated by Ahmad in his Musnad.] Also, regarding the virtue of this tremendous day, we have the hadith related by ʿĀ'ishah ﵂ that the Messenger of Allah ﷺ said, 'There is not a day in which Allah emancipates from the Fire more slaves [Muslims] than the Day of ʿArafah, and verily He draws near [a metaphor for His honouring His pilgrims and not to be taken literally as Allah does not resemble His creation in any manner whatsoever] and then boasts about them to His angels.' ʿItr, Nūr al-Dīn. *al-Ḥajj wa al-ʿumrah fi al-fiqh al-Islāmī*, 220.

اَللَّهُمَّ إِلَيْكَ تَوَجَّهْتُ ، وَوَجْهَكَ الْكَرِيْمَ أَرَدْتُ ، فَاجْعَلْ ذَنْبِي مَغْفُوْراً، وَحَجِّيْ مَبْرُوْراً، وَارْحَمْنِيْ إِنَّكَ عَلَى كُلِّ شَيْءٍ قَدِيْرٌ.

O Allah, to You I have turned, and Your noble countenance I seek, so make my sin a forgiven one and my pilgrimage an accepted one and have mercy on me. Verily, You have power over everything.

Profusely chant the *talbiyah*, and likewise recite the Qur'an, the rest of the invocations, supplications and the words,

رَبَّنَا آتِنَا فِي الدُّنْيَا حَسَنَةً وَفِي الْآخِرَةِ حَسَنَةً وَقِنَا عَذَابَ النَّارِ.

O our Lord, give us good in this world and good in the next world, and guard us from the torment of the Fire.

When one's gaze falls on the Mountain of Mercy [in 'Arafah],[108] glorify Allah, invoke 'Allah is the greatest' (*takbīr*) and 'There is no deity except Allah' (*tahlīl*) and seek His forgiveness. It is a sunnah for one to wash oneself in preparation for the rituals in 'Arafah and to initially proceed towards the Namirah mosque, in order to listen to the sermon and perform the *ẓuhr* and *'aṣr* prayers combined behind the General Imam.[109]

---

108 [T] It is better to stand near the mountain where the Prophet ﷺ stood, on the big black rocks that are laid on the floor, if convenient. As for climbing the Mount of Mercy itself, as some ignorant people do, then it is not legislated. 'Itr, Nūr al-Dīn. *al-Ḥajj wa al-'umrah fi al-fiqh al-Islāmī*, 219.

109 [T] The imam appointed by the Muslim ruler to deliver the sermons during hajj and lead the pilgrims in prayers.

THE SUPPLICATIONS IN ʿARAFAH

بِسْمِ اللهِ الرَّحْمَنِ الرَّحِيْمِ . أَلْحَمْدُ للهِ رَبِّ الْعَالَـمِيْنَ.
الرَّحْمَنِ الرَّحِيْمِ ...آمِيْنَ.

In the name of Allah, the All-Merciful, the Compassionate. All praise belongs to Allah, the Lord of the Worlds, the All-Merciful, the Compassionate ... Āmīn.

اَللَّهُمَّ صَلِّ عَلَى سَيِّدِنَا مُحَمَّدٍ وَعَلَى آلِ سَيِّدِنَا مُحَمَّدٍ ،
كَمَـا صَلَّيْتَ عَلَى سَيِّدِنَا إِبْرَاهِيْمَ ...

O Allah, send Your reverential mercy upon our master Muhammad and the family of our master Muhammad, just as send Your reverential mercy upon our master Ibrāhīm ...

اَللَّهُمَّ لَكَ الْحَمْدُ كَالَّذِيْ تَقُوْلُ وَخَيْرًا مِمَّا نَقُوْلُ ، اَللَّهُمَّ لَكَ
صَلَاتِيْ وَنُسُكِيْ وَمَحْيَايَ وَمَمَاتِيْ . وَإِلَيْكَ مَآبِيْ ، وَلَكَ رَبِّ تُرَاثِيْ ،
اَللَّهُمَّ إِنِّيْ أَعُوْذُ بِكَ مِنْ عَذَابِ الْقَبْرِ ، وَوَسْوَسَةِ الصَّدْرِ، وَشَتَاتِ
الْأَمْرِ، اَللَّهُمَّ إِنِّيْ أَعُوْذُ بِكَ مِنْ شَرِّ مَا تَجِيْءُ بِهِ الرِّيْحُ.

O Allah, to You belongs all praise, as You say and better than what we say. O Allah, for You is my prayer, my rites and my life and death. To You is my return, and to You, my Lord, belongs my inheritance and wealth. O Allah, I take refuge in You from the torment in the grave, [satanic] whisperings within my chest and from disarray. O Allah, verily I take refuge in You from the evil of what the wind brings.

اَللَّهُمَّ رَبَّنَا تَقَبَّلْ مِنَّا إِنَّكَ أَنْتَ السَّمِيْعُ الْعَلِيْمُ ، رَبَّنَا وَاجْعَلْنَا مُسْلِمَيْنِ لَكَ وَمِنْ ذُرِّيَّتِنَا أُمَّةً مُسْلِمَةً لَكَ وَأَرِنَا مَنَاسِكَنَا وَتُبْ عَلَيْنَا إِنَّكَ أَنْتَ التَّوَّابُ الرَّحِيْمُ.

O Allah, our Lord, accept from us. Verily, You are the All-Hearing, the All-Knowing. Our Lord, and make us from amongst those who submit themselves to you [Muslims] and from our progeny a nation that submits itself to you, and show us our rites and accept our repentance. Verily, You are the Oft-Accepter of Repentance, the Compassionate.

رَبَّنَا آتِنَا فِي الدُّنْيَا حَسَنَةً وَفِي الْآخِرَةِ حَسَنَةً وَقِنَا عَذَابَ النَّارِ.

Our Lord, give us good in this world and good in the next world, and guard us from the torment of the Fire.

اَللَّهُمَّ رَبَّنَا لَا تُؤَاخِذْنَا إِنْ نَسِيْنَا أَوْ أَخْطَأْنَا، رَبَّنَا وَلَا تَحْمِلْ عَلَيْنَا إِصْراً كَمَا حَمَلْتَهُ عَلَى الَّذِيْنَ مِنْ قَبْلِنَا، رَبَّنَا وَلَا تُحَمِّلْنَا مَا لَا طَاقَةَ لَنَا بِهِ، وَاعْفُ عَنَّا، وَاغْفِرْ لَنَا، وَارْحَمْنَا ، أَنْتَ مَوْلَانَا فَانْصُرْنَا عَلَى الْقَوْمِ الْكَافِرِيْنَ.

O Allah, our Lord, do not hold it against us if we forget or err. Our Lord, do not burden us with a weighty command as You burdened those before us. Our Lord, do not hold us responsible for that over which we do not have power, and pardon us, forgive us, and have mercy on us. You are our master, so grant us victory over the disbelieving folk.

رَبَّنَا لَا تُزِغْ قُلُوْبَنَا بَعْدَ إِذْ هَدَيْتَنَا وَهَبْ لَنَا مِنْ لَدُنْكَ رَحْمَةً إِنَّكَ أَنْتَ الْوَهَّابُ.

Our Lord, do not allow our hearts to deviate after having guided us, and grant us from Yourself a mercy. Verily, You are the Benevolent.

رَبِّ هَبْ لِيْ مِن لَّدُنْكَ ذُرِّيَّةً طَيِّبَةً إِنَّكَ سَمِيْعُ الدُّعَاء.

My Lord, grant me from Yourself a pure progeny. Verily, You are the Hearer of Supplications.

رَبَّنَا اغْفِرْ لَنَا ذُنُوْبَنَا وَإِسْرَافَنَا فِيْ أَمْرِنَا ، وَثَبِّتْ أَقْدَامَنَا ، وَانْصُرْنَا عَلَى الْقَوْمِ الْكَافِرِيْنَ.

Our Lord, forgive our sins and our excessiveness in our affairs. Make firm our feet, and grant us victory over the disbelieving folk.

رَبَّنَا ظَلَمْنَا أَنفُسَنَا وَإِنْ لَمْ تَغْفِرْ لَنَا وَتَرْحَمْنَا لَنَكُوْنَنَّ مِنَ الْخَاسِرِيْنَ.

Our Lord, we have wronged ourselves, and if You do not forgive us and have mercy on us, we shall surely be from amongst the losers.

اَللَّهُمَّ رَبَّنَا أَنْتَ مَوْلَانَا فَاغْفِرْ لَنَا وَارْحَمْنَا وَأَنْتَ خَيْرُ الرَّاحِمِيْنَ ، وَاكْتُبْ لَنَا فِيْ هَـٰذِهِ الدُّنْيَا حَسَنَةً وَفِي الْآخِرَةِ ، إِنَّا هُدْنَا إِلَيْكَ.

O Allah, our Lord, You are our master, so forgive us and have mercy on us, as You are the best of those who show mercy; and decree good for us in this world and in the next world. Verily, we have been guided to You.

اَللَّهُمَّ رَبَّنَا آتِنَا مِنْ لَّدُنْكَ رَحْمَةً وَهَيِّئْ لَنَا مِنْ أَمْرِنَا رَشَداً.

O Allah, our Lord, grant us a mercy from Yourself, and facilitate for us a right course in our affairs.

رَبِّ اشْرَحْ لِيْ صَدْرِيْ وَيَسِّرْ لِيْ أَمْرِيْ وَاحْلُلْ عُقْدَةً مِنْ لِّسَانِيْ
يَفْقَهُوْا قَوْلِيْ ، وَاجْعَلْ لِيْ وَزِيْراً مِنْ أَهْلِيْ.

My Lord, open my heart, facilitate for me that with which You have commanded me, and untie a knot [impediment] from my tongue so that they understand what I say, and assign for me an aide from my family.

رَبِّ أَعُوْذُ بِكَ مِنْ هَمَزَاتِ الشَّيَاطِيْنِ وَأَعُوْذُ بِكَ
رَبِّ أَنْ يَحْضُرُوْنَ.

My Lord, I take refuge in You from the whisperings of the devils, and I take refuge in You, my Lord, lest they come near me.

رَبَّنَا اصْرِفْ عَنَّا عَذَابَ جَهَنَّمَ ، إِنَّ عَذَابَهَا كَانَ غَرَامًا ،
إِنَّهَا سَاءَتْ مُسْتَقَرًّا وَمُقَاماً.

Our Lord, avert from us the torment of Hellfire, for verily its torment is a grave loss; verily, what a bad place of settlement and residence it is.

رَبَّنَا هَبْ لَنَا مِنْ أَزْوَاجِنَا وَذُرِّيَّاتِنَا قُرَّةَ أَعْيُنٍ
وَاجْعَلْنَا لِلْمُتَّقِيْنَ إِمَامًا.

Our Lord, grant us from our spouses and offspring happiness, and make us for the God-conscious a leader.

رَبِّ هَبْ لِيْ حُكْمًا وَأَلْحِقْنِيْ بِالصَّالِحِيْنَ ، وَاجْعَلْ لِّيْ لِسَانَ
صِدْقٍ فِي الْآخِرِيْنَ ، وَاجْعَلْنِيْ مِنْ وَرَثَةِ جَنَّةِ النَّعِيْم.

My Lord, grant me correct judgement [knowledge or wisdom], join me with the righteous, grant me good repute among the righteous, and make me from amongst the inheritors of the Garden of Bliss.

اَللَّهُمَّ رَبَّنَا اغْفِرْ لَنَا وَلِإِخْوَانِنَا الَّذِيْنَ سَبَقُوْنَا بِالْإِيْمَانِ ، وَلَا تَجْعَلْ
فِيْ قُلُوْبِنَا غِلًّا لِّلَّذِيْنَ آمَنُوْا ، رَبَّنَا إِنَّكَ رَؤُوْفٌ رَحِيْمٌ.

O Allah, our Lord, forgive us and our brothers who have preceded us in faith, and do not place in our hearts rancour for those who believe. Our Lord, verily You are compassionate, merciful.

اَللَّهُمَّ رَبَّنَا أَتْمِمْ لَنَا نُوْرَنَا وَاغْفِرْ لَنَا إِنَّكَ عَلَى كُلِّ شَيْءٍ قَدِيْرٌ.

O Allah, our Lord, complete for us our light, and forgive us. Verily, You have power over everything.

اَللَّهُمَّ أَنْتَ رَبِّيْ لَا إِلَهَ إِلَّا أَنْتَ ، خَلَقْتَنِيْ وَأَنَا عَبْدُكَ ، وَأَنَا عَلَى
عَهْدِكَ وَوَعْدِكَ مَا اسْتَطَعْتُ ، أَعُوْذُ بِكَ مِنْ شَرِّ مَا صَنَعْتُ ،
أَبُوْءُ لَكَ بِنِعْمَتِكَ عَلَيَّ وَأَبُوْءُ بِذَنْبِيْ فَاغْفِرْ لِيْ ،
فَإِنَّهُ لَا يَغْفِرُ الذُّنُوْبَ إِلَّا أَنْتَ.

O Allah, You are my Lord. There is no deity except You. You created me, and I am your slave, and I continue to adhere to [my] covenant and promise to You as much as I can. I take refuge in You from the evil of what I have done. I acknowledge the favours You have bestowed upon me and acknowledge my sin; so forgive me, as there is none who forgives sins except You.

اَللَّهُمَّ إِنِّيْ أَسْلَمْتُ نَفْسِيْ إِلَيْكَ ، وَفَوَّضْتُ أَمْرِيْ إِلَيْكَ ، وَأَلْجَأْتُ
ظَهْرِيْ إِلَيْكَ ، رَهْبَةً وَرَغْبَةً إِلَيْكَ ، لَامَلْجَأَ وَلَا مَنْجَا مِنْكَ
إِلَّا إِلَيْكَ ، آمَنْتُ بِكِتَابِكَ الَّذِيْ أَنْزَلْتَ وَنَبِيِّكَ الَّذِيْ أَرْسَلْتَ.

O Allah, I have surrendered myself to You, consigned my affair to You, and entrusted my back to You,[110] *out of awe and desire for You. There is no refuge or escape from You except to You. I have believed in Your Book which You have revealed, and Your Prophet whom You have sent.*

110 [T] A metaphor for relying on Him for support.

اَللَّهُمَّ لَكَ الْحَمْدُ أَنْتَ نُوْرُ السَّمَوَاتِ وَالْأَرْضِ وَمَنْ فِيْهِنَّ ، وَلَكَ الْحَمْدُ أَنْتَ قَيِّمُ السَّمَوَاتِ وَالْأَرْضِ وَمَنْ فِيْهِنَّ ، وَلَكَ الْحَمْدُ أَنْتَ الْحَقُّ ، وَوَعْدُكَ حَقٌّ ، وَقَوْلُكَ حَقٌّ ، وَلِقَاؤُكَ حَقٌّ ، وَالْجَنَّةُ حَقٌّ ، وَالنَّارُ حَقٌّ ، وَالسَّاعَةُ حَقٌّ ، وَالنَّبِيُّوْنَ حَقٌّ ، وَمُحَمَّدٌ حَقٌّ ، اَللَّهُمَّ لَكَ أَسْلَمْتُ ، وَعَلَيْكَ تَوَكَّلْتُ ، وَبِكَ آمَنْتُ وَإِلَيْكَ أَنَبْتُ ، وَبِكَ خَاصَمْتُ ، وَإِلَيْكَ حَاكَمْتُ ، فَاغْفِرْلِيْ مَا قَدَّمْتُ، وَمَا أَخَّرْتُ ، وَمَا أَسْرَرْتُ ، وَمَا أَعْلَنْتُ ، أَنْتَ الْـمُقَدِّمُ وَأَنْتَ الْـمُؤَخِّرُ، لَا إِلَهَ إِلَّا أَنْتَ.

O Allah, to You belongs all praise, and You are the light of the heavens, the earth and whoever is therein. To You belongs all praise. You are the sustainer of the heavens, the earth and whoever is therein. To You belongs all praise. You are true, Your promise is true, Your word is true, Your meeting is true; Paradise is true, the Fire is true, the hour is true, and the prophets are true, and Muhammad is true. O Allah, to You I have submitted; in You I have placed my trust; in You I have believed; to You I have returned; by You I argue my case, and to You I turn to for arbitration; so forgive me for what I have done in the past and whatever I do in the future, and whatever I have done in private, and whatever I have done in public. You are the one who promotes, and You are the one who demotes. There is no deity except You.

رَبِّ اغْفِرْ لِيْ خَطِيْئَتِيْ وَجَهْلِيْ ، وَإِسْرَافِيْ فِيْ أَمرِيْ كُلِّهِ ، وَمَا أَنْتَ
أَعْلَمُ بِهِ مِنِّىْ ، اَللَّهُمَّ اغْفِرْ لِيْ خَطَايَاىَ ، وَعَمَدِيْ ، وَجَهْلِي ،
وَجِدِّيْ ، وَهَزْلِيْ ، وَكُلُّ ذَلِكَ عِنْدِيْ.

My Lord, forgive me my wrongdoings and ignorance, my excessiveness in all of my affairs, and that which You are better aware of than me. O Allah, forgive me my mistakes, my deliberate [sins], [those done out of] my ignorance and jest, and I take responsibility for all of that.

اَللَّهُمَّ إِنِّيْ أَعُوْذُ بِكَ مِنْ فِتْنَةِ النَّارِ، وَعَذَابِ النَّارِ، وَفِتْنَةِ الْقَبْرِ
وَعَذَابِ الْقَبرِ ، وَشَرِّ فِتْنَةِ الْغِنَى ، وَشرِّ فِتْنَةِ الْفَقْرِ، اَللَّهُمَّ إِنِّيْ أَعُوْذُ
بِكَ مِنْ شَرِّ فِتْنَةِ الْمَسِيْحِ الدَّجَّالِ، اَللَّهُمَّ اغْسِلْ قَلْبِيْ بِمَاءِ الثَّلْجِ
وَالْبَرَدِ ، اَللَّهُمَّ إِنِّيْ أَعُوْذُ بِكَ مِنَ الْكَسَلِ وَالْمَأْثَمِ وَالْمَغْرَمِ.

O Allah, verily I take refuge in You from the tribulation of the Fire, the torment of the Fire, the tribulation in the grave, the torment in the grave, the evil of tribulation in wealth and the evil of tribulation in poverty. O Allah, verily I take refuge in You from the tribulation of the evil of the false messiah. O Allah, wash my heart with water from snow and hail. O Allah, I take refuge in You from laziness, committing sins and incurring loss.

لَا إِلَٰـهَ إِلَّا اللهُ الْعَظِيْمُ الْحَلِيْمُ ، لَا إِلَٰـهَ إِلَّا اللهُ رَبُّ الْعَرْشِ الْعَظِيْمِ ، لَا إِلَٰـهَ إِلَّا اللهُ رَبُّ السَّمَوَاتِ ، وَرَبُّ الْأَرْضِ ، وَرَبُّ الْعَرْشِ الْكَرِيْمِ.

There is no deity except Allah, the Almighty, the Forbearing. There is no deity except Allah, the Lord of the Grand Throne. There is no deity except Allah, the Lord of the Heavens, the Lord of the Earth and the Lord of the Splendid Throne.

لَا إِلَٰـهَ إِلَّا اللهُ وَحْدَهُ لَا شَرِيْكَ لَهُ ، اللهُ أَكْبَرُ كَبِيْراً ، وَالْحَمْدُ لِلّٰـهِ كَثِيْراً ، سُبْحَانَ اللهِ رَبِّ الْعَالَمِيْنَ ، لَا حَوْلَ وَلَا قُوَّةَ إِلَّا بِاللهِ الْعَزِيْزِ الْحَكِيْمِ ، اَللّٰهُمَّ اغْفِرْ لِيْ وَارْحَمْنِيْ وَاهْدِنِيْ وَعَافِنِيْ وَارْزُقْنِيْ.

There is no deity except Allah alone; He has no partner. Allah is the greatest—in abundance, and all praise belongs to Allah—in tremendousness. Glory be to Allah, the Lord of the Worlds. There is no power or might except through Allah, the Almighty, the Wise. O Allah, forgive me, have mercy on me, guide me, protect me and provide for me.

اَللّٰهُمَّ اقْضِ عَنِّيَ الدَّيْنَ ، وَأَغْنِنِيْ مِنَ الْفَقْرِ ، وَأَمْتِعْنِيْ بِسَمْعِيْ وَبَصَرِيْ وَمَلَكَاتِيْ مَا أَحْيَيْتَنِيْ ، وَاجْعَلْهُ الْوَارِثَ مِنِّيْ.

O Allah, discharge my debts on my behalf, enrich me from poverty, allow me to enjoy my hearing, sight and faculties as long as you keep me alive and make them an inheritor of mine [i.e. allow these faculties to accompany me till death].

اَللَّهُمَّ إِنِّيْ أَسْأَلُكَ الثَّبَاتَ فِي الْأَمْرِ، وَالْعَزِيْمَةَ عَلَى الرُّشْدِ ، وَأَسْأَلُكَ شُكْرَ نِعْمَتِكَ ، وَحُسْنَ عِبَادَتِكَ ، وَأَسْأَلُكَ لِسَاناً صَادِقاً وَ قَلْباً سَلِيْمـاً ، وَأَعُوْذُ بِكَ مِنْ شَرِّ مَا تَعْلَمُ ، وَأَسْأَلُكَ مِنْ خَيْرِ مَا تَعْلَمُ ، وَأَسْتَغْفِرُكَ مِمَّا تَعْلَمُ ، إِنَّكَ أَنْتَ عَلَّامُ الْغُيُوْبِ.

O Allah, verily I ask You for fortitude in religion [literally, the affair] and steadfastness upon guidance. I ask You [to enable me to show] gratitude for Your blessings and that I worship You well. I ask You for a truthful tongue and a sound heart. I take refuge in You from the evil of what You know, and I ask You for the best of what You know, and I seek Your forgiveness for that which You know. Verily, You are All-Knowing of the Unseen.

اَللَّهُمَّ إِنِّيْ أَسْأَلُكَ رَحْمَةً مِنْ عِنْدِكَ تَهْدِيْ بِهَا قَلْبِيْ ، وَتَجْمَعُ بِهَا أَمْرِيْ ، وَتُصْلِحُ بِهَا غَائِبِيْ وَتَرْفَعُ بِهَا شَاهِدِيْ ، وَتُزَكِّيْ بِهَا عَمَلِيْ، وَتُلْهِمُنِيْ بِهَا رُشْدِيْ ، وَتَرُدُّ بِهَا أُلْفَتِيْ ، وَتَعْصِمُنِيْ بِهَا مِنْ كُلِّ سُوْءٍ ، اَللَّهُمَّ أَعْطِنِيْ إِيْمَـاناً وَيَقِيْناً لَيْسَ بَعْدَهُ كُفْرٌ ، وَرَحْمَةً أَنَالُ بِهَا شَرَفَ كَرَامَتِكَ فِي الدُّنْيَا وَالْآخِرَةِ ، أَسْأَلُكَ يَا قَاضِيَ الْأُمُوْرِ، وَيَا شَافِيَ الصُّدُوْرِ أَنْ تُجِيْرَنِيْ مِنْ عَذَابِ السَّعِيْرِ وَمِنْ دَعْوَةِ

الثُّبُوْرِ. أَسْأَلُكَ الْأَمْنَ يَوْمَ الْوَعِيْدِ ، وَالْجَنَّةَ يَوْمَ الْخُلُوْدِ ، مَعَ الْـمُقَرَّبِيْنَ الشُّهُوْدِ ، اَللَّهُمَّ اجْعَلْنَا هَادِيْنَ مُهْتَدِيْنَ ، غَيْرَ ضَالِّيْنَ وَلَا مُضِلِّيْنَ ، سِلْمـاً لِأَوْلِيَائِكَ ، وَعَدُوّاً لِأَعْدَائِكَ.

O Allah, verily I ask You for a mercy from Yourself by which You guide my heart, rectify my affair(s), mend my internal traits, raise my external good deeds [for acceptance], purify my deed and inspire me [to] my guidance, return my harmony, and protect me from all evil. O Allah, grant me faith and certainty that is free of any disbelief, and a mercy by which I attain the honour of Your grace in this world and the next. I ask You, O Fulfiller of Needs and Healer of Hearts, that you protect me from the torment of the Hellfire and from calling out for destruction.[111] *I ask You for security on the Day of the Threat and Paradise on the Day of Eternity, with those who are drawn near [to Allah] and behold [Him]. O Allah, make us guides and guided, not misguided and misguiding, allies of Your friends and enemies of Your enemies.*

اَللَّهُمَّ هَـٰذَا الدُّعَاءُ وَعَلَيْكَ الْإِجَابَةُ ، وَهَـٰذَا الْجَهْدُ وَعَلَيْكَ التُّكْلَانُ. اَللَّهُمَّ اجْعَلْ لِيْ نُوْراً فِيْ قَلْبِيْ ، وَنُوْراً فِيْ قَبْرِيْ ، وَنُوْراً مِنْ بَيْنَ يَدَيَّ ، وَنُوْراً مِنْ خَلْفِيْ ، وَنُوْراً عَنْ يَمِيْنِيْ ، وَنُوْراً عَنْ

111 [T] That is when the inhabitants of the Hellfire can no longer bear the punishment.

شِمَـالِيْ ، وَنُوْراً مِنْ فَوْقِيْ ، وَنُوْراً مِنْ تَحْتِيْ ، وَنُوْراً فِيْ سَمْعِيْ ، وَنُوْراً فِيْ بَصَرِيْ، وَنُوْراً فِيْ شَعْرِيْ ، وَنُوْراً فِيْ بَشَرِيْ ، وَنُوْراً فِيْ لَحْمِيْ ، وَنُوْراً فِيْ دَمِيْ ، وَنُوْراً فِيْ عِظَامِيْ ، اَللَّهُمَّ أَعْظِمْ لِيْ نُوْراً، وَأَعْطِنِيْ نُوْراً، وَاجْعَلْ لِيْ نُوْراً ، سُبْحَانَ ذِي الْفَضْلِ وَالنِّعَمِ ، سُبْحَانَ ذِي الْـمَجْدِ وَالْكَرَمِ سُبْحَان ذِي الْجَلَالِ وَالْإِكْرَامِ.

O Allah, this is the supplication and upon You is the response, and this is the endeavour and upon You is the reliance. O Allah, make for me a light in my heart, a light in my grave, a light before me, a light behind me, a light on my right, a light on my left, a light above me, a light beneath me, a light in my hearing, a light in my sight, a light in my hair, a light in my skin, a light in my flesh, a light in my blood and a light in my bones. O Allah, magnify for me my light, grant me a light and make for me a light. Glory be to the possessor of bounty and favours. Glory be to the possessor of magnificence and generosity. Glory be to the possessor of majesty and benevolence.

اَللَّهُمَّ أَنْتَ الْـمَلِكُ لَا إِلَهَ إِلَّا أَنْتَ ، أَنْتَ رَبِّيْ خَلَقْتَنِيْ وَأَنَا عَبْدُكَ، ظَلَمْتُ نَفْسِيْ وَاعْتَرَفْتُ بِذَنْبِيْ فَاغْفِرْ لِيْ ذَنْبِيْ جَمِيْعاً إِنَّهُ لَا يَغْفِرُ الذُّنُوْبَ إِلَّا أَنْتَ ، وَاهْدِنِيْ لِأَحْسَنِ الْأَخْلَاقِ ، لَا يَهْدِيْ لِأَحْسَنِهَا إِلَّا أَنْتَ ، وَاصْرِفْ عَنِّيْ سَيِّئَهَا لَا يَصْرِفُ عَنِّيْ سَيِّئَهَا إِلَّا أَنْتَ ، لَبَّيْكَ وَسَعْدَيْكَ وَالْخَيْرُ كُلُّهُ فِيْ يَدَيْكَ وَالشَّرُّ لَيْسَ إِلَيْكَ، أَنَا بِكَ وَإِلَيْكَ ، تَبَارَكْتَ وَتَعَالَيْتَ أَسْتَغْفِرُكَ وَأَتُوْبُ إِلَيْكَ.

O Allah, You are the sovereign. There is no deity except You. You are my Lord. You created me and I am Your slave. I have wronged myself and acknowledge my sin, so forgive me all my sins, as there is none who forgives sins except You, and guide me to the best of character traits, as none guides to the best of them except You, and avert from me the worst of them, as none averts from me the worst of them except You. Ever at Your service, and ever happy to be at Your service. All goodness is in Your hands [i.e. possession], while evil is not attributed to You. I am from You and [returning] to You. You are Transcendent and Exalted. I seek Your forgiveness and repent to You.

اَللَّهُمَّ اغْفِرْ لِيْ ذَنْبِيْ، وَوَسِّعْ لِيْ فِيْ دَارِيْ، وَبَارِكْ لِيْ فِيْمَا رَزَقْتَنِيْ.

O Allah, forgive me my sins, make expansive for me my abode, and bless me in whatever You have provided me.

اَللَّهُمَّ مَا قَصَّرَ عَنْهُ رَأْيِيْ ، وَلَمْ تَبْلُغْهُ نِيَّتِيْ ، وَلَمْ تَبْلُغْهُ مَسْأَلَتِيْ مِنْ خَيْرٍ وَعَدْتَهُ أَحَداً مِنْ خَلْقِكَ ، أَوْ خَيْرٍ أَنْتَ مُعْطِيْهِ أَحَداً مِنْ عِبَادِكَ ، فَإِنِّيْ أَرْغَبُ إِلَيْكَ فِيْهِ ، وَأَسْأَلُكَ إِيَّاهُ بِرَحْمَتِكَ يَارَبَّ الْعَالَمِيْنَ.

O Allah, whatever good that You have promised to any of Your creation or that You will give to any of Your slaves which my thoughts fell short of, or where my intention and request failed to achieve, then indeed

I ask You for it, and I ask You for it by Your mercy, O Lord of the Worlds.

اَللَّهُمَّ رَبَّنَا آتِنَا فِي الدُّنْيَا حَسَنَةً وَفِي الْآخِرَةِ حَسَنَةً وَقِنَا عَذَابَ النَّارِ. رَبَّنَا تَقَبَّلْ مِنَّا إِنَّكَ أَنْتَ السَّمِيْعُ الْعَلِيْمُ.

O Allah, our Lord, give us good in this world good and good in the next world, and guard us from the torment of the Fire. Our Lord, accept from us. You are the All-Hearing, the All-Knowing.

بِسْمِ اللهِ الرَّحْمَـٰنِ الرَّحِيْمِ. أَلْحَمْدُ لِلّٰـهِ رَبِّ الْعَالَـمِيْنَ. أَلرَّحْمَـٰنِ الرَّحِيْمِ ...آمِيْنَ.

In the name of Allah, the All-Merciful, the Compassionate. All praise is due to Allah, the Lord of the Worlds, the All-Merciful, the Compassionate ... Āmīn.

اَللَّهُمَّ صَلِّ عَلَى سَيِّدِنَا مُحَمَّدٍ وَعَلَى آلِ سَيِّدِنَا مُحَمَّدٍ، كَمَـا صَلَّيْتَ عَلَى سَيِّدِنَا إِبْرَاهِيْمَ ...

O Allah, send Your reverential mercy upon our master Muhammad and the family of our master Muhammad, just as You sent Your reverential mercy upon our master Ibrāhīm ...

وَسَلَامٌ عَلَى الْـمُرْسَلِيْنَ وَالْحَمْدُ لِلّٰـهِ رَبِّ الْعَالَـمِيْنَ.

And peace be upon the messengers, and all praise is due to Allah, the Lord of the Worlds.

Continue, dear pilgrim, standing in this state until sunset, and beware of departing ʿArafah before sunset, because if one were to pass the boundaries of ʿArafah before sunset, it would become necessary for one to offer a sacrifice.[112] Do not perform the sunset prayer in ʿArafah; instead, it is compulsory for one to postpone it, so that one performs it with the nightfall prayer in al-Muzdalifah.

Setting off for al-Muzdalifah and spending the night therein

When the sun sets on the Day of ʿArafah and its rays completely disappear, proceed towards al-Muzdalifah, for the Prophet ﷺ left ʿArafah after sunset when the sun's rays had completely disappeared; he ﷺ was riding his camel, travelling on it steadily and hastening whenever he would find space. Profusely chant the *talbiyah*—as al-Muzdalifah is amongst the most emphasised of places where it is to be chanted—and [profusely] recite the Qur'an and supplicate.

It is recommended that one profusely recite en-route [the invocation],

لَا إِلَٰهَ إِلَّا اللهُ وَ اللهُ أَكْبَرُ.

There is no deity except Allah. Allah is the greatest.

112 Standing in ʿArafah till sunset is a sunnah according to the Shāfiʿīs and Ḥanbalīs, whereas according to the Mālikīs, the hajj is invalidated [if one leaves before sunset], unless one returns to ʿArafah.

And also recite en-route,

إِلَيْكَ اللَّهُمَّ أَرْغَبُ ، وَإِيَّاكَ أَرْجُوْ ، فَتَقَبَّلْ نُسُكِيْ وَوَفِّقْنِيْ وَارْزُقْنِيْ فِيْهِ مِنَ الْخَيْرِ أَكْثَرَ مَا أَطْلُبُ ، وَلَا تُخَيِّبْنِيْ إِنَّكَ أَنْتَ اللهُ الْجَوَّادُ الْكَرِيْمُ.

It is You, O Allah, I seek, and in You I place my hopes, so accept my rites, grant me success and provide me therein of goodness more than what I can ask, and do not disappoint me. Verily, You are Allah, the Generous, the Benevolent.

Alight close to al-Mashʿar al-Ḥarām (Mount Quzaḥ) if it is feasible for one; it is apparent and well known, and a great mosque, upon which is a minaret with bright lights, has been built over its site as a landmark for people; so head towards the mosque if you are able. Then hasten to perform the *maghrib* and *ʿishā'* prayers as a delayed combination; it is not conditional for the validity of this combination that it be performed in congregation with the imam of hajj; rather, it is valid by consensus, even if performed individually, though one loses out on the reward of praying in congregation. Also, delay the sunnah of the *maghrib* prayer until after the obligatory *ʿishā'* prayer.

Spending the night in al-Muzdalifah is a sunnah.[113] The entire place of al-Muzdalifah is valid for one to make the

---

113 According to the Shāfiʿīs and Ḥanbalīs it is necessary to spend some time in al-Muzdalifah after midnight, even if it is short; whereas according to the Mālikīs it is necessary to spend any portion of the night in al-Muzdalifah for the duration it takes to dismount from a camel and take the luggage off its back.

stay, except Wādi Muḥassir, which separates it from Minā; so know and bear that in mind. Additionally, spend that night supplicating, reciting invocations and chanting the *talbiyah*, for this is the night of Eid.

Standing in al-Muzdalifah

Lie down till just before dawn, as did the Prophet ﷺ, and thereafter prepare for the standing, as staying in al-Muzdalifah after dawn, even for a short while, is necessary.[114] Beseech Allah by supplicating, and have a strong expectation of its acceptance, for the site of standing in al-Mashʿar al-Ḥarām is one of proximity to Allah Most High and honour for a pilgrim after his standing in ʿArafah. Moreover, do not forget the *takbīr*s of the two Eids after the *fajr* prayer and the rest of the prayers, because their time then commences.[115]

THE SUPPLICATIONS IN AL-MUZDALIFAH

Allah Most High has said: *Then when you depart from ʿArafah, remember Allah at al-Mashʿar al-Ḥarām, and remember Him just as He guided you* [Qur'an 2:198]. The following are amongst the supplications that have been mentioned for the occasion:

---

114 It is a sunnah according to other than the Ḥanafīs.

115 [T] It is necessary to recite them once after each obligatory prayer, from the *fajr* prayer on the Day of ʿArafah until after the ʿ*aṣr* prayer on the thirteenth Dhu al-Ḥijjah; they are the words *Allāhu akbar, Allāhu akbar, lā ilāha illa llāhu wallāhu akbar, wa lillāhi l-ḥamd* (Allah is the greatest; Allah is the greatest. There is no deity [worthy of worship] except Allah. Allah is the greatest, and to Allah belongs all praise).

اَللَّهُمَّ إِنِّيْ أَسْأَلُكَ فَوَاتِحَ الْخَيْرِ، وَخَوَاتِمَهُ ، وَجَوَامِعَهُ ،
وَأَوَّلَهُ وَآخِرَهُ ، وَظَاهِرَهُ وَبَاطِنَهُ ، وَالدَّرَجَاتِ الْعُلَى فِي الْجَنَّةِ ،
وَأَنْ تُصْلِحَ لِيْ شَأْنِيْ كُلَّهُ ، وَأَنْ تَصْرِفَ عَنِّيَ الشَّرَّ كُلَّهُ ،
فَإِنَّهُ لَا يَفْعَلُ ذَلِكَ غَيْرُكَ وَلَا يَجُوْدُ بِهِ إِلَّا أَنْتَ.

O Allah, I ask You for the openings of goodness, and its endings and completeness, its first and last, its manifest and hidden, and elevated degrees in Paradise; and that You improve all of my affairs and ward off me all evil, as none can do that except You, and none gives it generously except You.

اَللَّهُمَّ لَكَ الْحَمْدُ كُلُّهُ ، وَلَكَ الْكَمَالُ كُلُّهُ ، وَلَكَ الْجَلَالُ كُلُّهُ ،
وَلَكَ التَّقْدِيْسُ كُلُّهُ ، اَللَّهُمَّ اغْفِرْ لِيْ جَمِيْعَ مَا أَسْلَفْتُهُ ، وَاعْصِمْنِيْ
فِيْمَا بَقِيَ ، وَارْزُقْنِيْ عَمَلاً صَالِحاً تَرْضَى بِهِ عَنِّيْ يَا ذَا الْفَضْلِ
الْعَظِيْمِ ، اَللَّهُمَّ إِنِّيْ أَسْتَشْفِعُ إِلَيْكَ بِخَوَاصِّ عِبَادِكَ ، وَأَتَوَسَّلُ
بِكَ إِلَيْكَ ، أَسْأَلُكَ أَنْ تَرْزُقَنِيْ جَوَامِعَ الْخَيْرِ كُلِّهِ ، وَأَنْ تَمُنَّ
عَلَيَّ بِمَا مَنَنْتَ عَلَى أَوْلِيَائِكَ ، وَأَنْ تُصْلِحَ حَالِيْ فِي
الْآخِرَةِ وَالدُّنْيَا يَا أَرْحَمَ الرَّاحِمِيْنَ.

O Allah, to You belongs all praise, all perfection, all majesty and all sanctity. O Allah, forgive me for all of what I have done in the past, protect me in that which remains [of my life] and grant me a righteous deed by which You will be pleased with me, O Possessor of tremendous bounty. O Allah, I seek intercession with

You by Your elite servants, and I ask by You to You; I ask You to provide me with comprehensive goodness, to favour me with what You have favoured Your friends and to improve my state in the next world and this world, O Most Merciful of the Merciful.

PICKING UP THE STONES

It is recommended that one pick up seven pebbles from al-Muzdalifah to throw at the site (*jamrah*) of ʿAqabah. Some Imams have recommended that one pick up seventy pebbles, so that there is enough to throw at all the sites, as picking up pebbles from the place where they are thrown at the sites is slightly offensive (*makrūh tanzīh*). It is recommended that one picks pebbles the size of pellets, and it is offensive to throw large stones. It is not valid to throw anything other than pebbles or matters defined as constituting a part of the earth [such as clay, bricks, soil or ceramics].

Travelling towards Minā

When it is daylight, leave al-Muzdalifah for Minā. It is a sunnah for one to depart before sunrise as did the Prophet ﷺ, in opposition to the idolaters.

Let one's utterances be the *talbiyah*, invocations and supplication, so profusely chant and recite them. Be fervent in chanting the *talbiyah* humbly, attentively, pleading and beseeching, as this is the end of its time, and one may not get another opportunity to chant a *talbiyah* in one's life.

When one reaches Minā, then supplicate,

أَلْحَمْدُ لِلّٰهِ الَّذِيْ بَلَّغَنِيْهَا سَالِمـاً مُعَافًى ، اَللّٰهُمَّ هٰـذِهِ مِنًى قَدْ
أَتَيْتُهَا وَأَنَا عَبْدُكَ وَ فِيْ قَبْضَتِكَ ، أَسْأَلُكَ أَنْ تَمُنَّ عَلَيَّ بِمَـا مَنَنْتَ
بِهِ عَلَى أَوْلِيَائِكَ ، اَللّٰهُمَّ إِنِّيْ أَعُوْذُ بِكَ مِنَ الْحِرْمَانِ ،
وَالْـمُصِيْبَةِ فِيْ دِيْنِيْ يَا أَرْحَمَ الرَّاحِمِيْنَ.

All praise belongs to Allah who has made me reach here safe and sound. O Allah, this is Minā that I have come to as Your slave and in Your grasp. I ask You to favour me with whatever You have favoured Your friends. O Allah, I take refuge in You from deprivation and misfortune in my religion, O Most Merciful of the Merciful.

The Day of Sacrifice

This day in Minā that one has now reached, my dear pilgrim, is the Day of Sacrifice, the day of the great Islamic festival, which Muslims celebrate by virtue of your performance of the hajj rituals, O pilgrim, so thank Allah for this blessing, be sincere to Him in all of your affairs and profusely invoke and supplicate to Him.

THE RITUALS IN MINĀ ON THE DAY OF SACRIFICE

These rituals are numerous and they are the following:

1. stoning the ʿAqabah site;
2. sacrificing [a sheep, camel or a cow];
3. shaving one's head [or cutting one's hair short];

4. the *Ṭawāf* of Departure (*Ṭawāf al-Ifāḍah*);
5. the *sa'y* (if one has not previously performed it).

We will explain these rituals as follows.

STONING THE 'AQABAH SITE (JAMRAH AL-'AQABAH)

It is necessary on this day to throw seven individual stones at the site of 'Aqabah only. The time for this stoning begins from dawn[116] on the Day of Sacrifice and lasts until dawn of the second day.[117]

The easiest time for stoning within this duration is an hour before sunset;[118] it is a time wherein lies no offence by the agreement of scholars, and similarly is the case with the rest of the days of stoning. It is recommended that one hasten in stoning immediately upon one's arrival, because when the Prophet ﷺ came to Minā he did not busy himself with anything until he stoned the site of 'Aqabah. The wisdom behind this stoning is that it is the greeting for Minā.

---

116 This is according to the Ḥanafīs and Mālikīs. According to the Shāfi'īs and Ḥanbalīs it is from midnight on the Day of Sacrifice; this [latter opinion] is easier for whoever is able, due to the reduction in congestion that results thereof.

117 And till sunset on the Day of Sacrifice according to the Mālikīs, while according to the Shāfi'īs and the Ḥanbalīs it lasts until the final day of *Tashrīq*.

118 [T]This was the case at the time when this work was written, which was in the nineties. However, since the expansion of the stoning sites with the construction of a five story bridge, numerous entrances and exits and separate roads for going to and fro from Mecca, it is now feasible to stone the sites quite comfortably throughout the day.

It is recommended to stand a distance of at least five arm spans away from the site, facing the site, with Minā on one's right and the road to Mecca on one's left. Then take a stone with one's right hand between the index finger and the thumb, raise the hand and throw the stones one after another.

In the course of throwing the stones, one should perceive that one is throwing away from oneself ignorance and condemnable traits, disgracing Satan and his party and humiliating them. Cease chanting the *talbiyah* with the first stone that one throws, busy oneself with chanting the *takbīr,* and recite the *takbīr* with every stone thrown in emulation of the Prophetic Sunnah:

بِسْمِ اللهِ وَاللهُ أَكْبَرُ، رَغْماً لِلشَّيْطَانِ وَحِزْبِهِ ، وَرِضاً لِلرَّحْمَـٰنِ.

In the name of Allah. Allah is the greatest. In humiliation of Satan and his party, and in [winning] the pleasure of the All-Merciful.

Throw the stones towards the site so that they fall within the circular wall surrounding the pillar. When one has finished throwing, depart without stopping, while reciting,

اَللَّهُمَّ اجْعَلْهُ حَجّاً مَبْرُوْراً ، وَسَعْياً مَشْكُوْراً ، وَذَنْباً مَغْفُوْراً.

O Allah, make it an accepted hajj, a rewarded endeavour and [my sin] a forgiven sin.

Profusely chant the *takbīr* during the Days of Sacrifice, as the *takbīr* is the formula during them.

THE SACRIFICE

Then go to the slaughter area to offer the sacrifice, as it is necessary for whoever performs umrah and hajj individually (*mutamatti*ʿ) or simultaneously (*qārin*). As for someone performing hajj only (*mufrid*), then neither the sacrificial offering nor the Eid sacrifice (*al-uḍḥiyyah*) is necessary for one; rather, it is recommended according to the Ḥanafis and others. So select a sheep that is free from defects and disabilities, plump and ample in meat, for that is considered reverence of Allah's symbols [of His religion], and resolve to show gratitude for Allah's blessings upon one and for Him enabling one to successfully perform hajj and umrah on a single journey. This sacrifice is in gratitude for His blessings and to redeem oneself from Allah's punishment. So lay down the animal to be sacrificed facing towards the qiblah, and recite in emulation of the sunnah,

وَجَّهْتُ وَجْهِيْ لِلَّذِيْ فَطَرَ السَّمَوَاتِ وَالْأَرْضَ حَنِيْفاً وَمَا أَنَا
مِنَ الْـمُشْرِكِيْنَ ، إِنَّ صَلَاتِيْ وَنُسُكِيْ وَمَحْيَايَ ، وَمَمَاتِيْ لله
رَبِّ الْعَالَـمِيْنَ ، لَا شَرِيْكَ لَهُ وَبِذَلِكَ أُمِرْتُ وَأَنَا
مِنَ الْـمُسْلِمِيْنَ. اَللَّهُمَّ مِنْكَ وَلَكَ.

I have turned my face towards the One Who has originated the heavens and the earth, naturally inclined towards true faith, and I am not of the idolaters. Verily, my prayer, devotional acts, life and death are for Allah, the Lord of the Worlds. He has no partner, and with that I have been commanded, and I am one of the Muslims. O Allah, from You and for You.

اَللَّهُمَّ تَقَبَّلْ مِنِّيْ (أَوْ مِنْ فُلَانٌ) بِسْمِ الله وَاللهُ أَكْبَرُ.

O Allah, accept from me or from So-and-so,' (if one is slaughtering on behalf of someone else). In the name of Allah. Allah is the greatest.

Give the slaughtered meat away in charity to the poor, eat from it and gift it to one's companions; unless the sacrifice was done due to a vow or was necessary as a means for redressing a violation committed during hajj, in which case it is necessary to give all of it away in charity: giving it away to the poor and not eating anything from it, and do not leave anything behind without giving it to the poor and giving them possession of it; so pay heed and do not be oblivious.

SHAVING OR SHORTENING THE HAIR

Thereafter, shave one's head or shorten one's hair [to the necessary level]. In this cutting of the hair here is a [token of] submission of one's affairs to Allah, and humbling oneself before Him; therefore, shaving with a blade is better than shortening the hair, due to the supplication transmitted from the Prophet ﷺ,

> O Allah, have mercy on those who shave their heads. So they [his companions] said, 'And what about those who shorten their hair, O Messenger of Allah?' To which he replied, 'O Allah, have mercy on those who shave their heads.' So they replied, 'And what about those who shorten their hair, O Messenger of

Allah?' To which he replied, 'And those who shorten their hair.'

The least amount necessary in shaving or cutting is a quarter of the head.[119] It is better that one not haggle with the barber over the price [of the haircut], and it is recommended for one to sit facing towards the qiblah, for the barber to begin with the right side of the head, followed by the left and for one to recite,

بِسْمِ اللهِ الرَّحْمَـٰنِ الرَّحِيْمِ ، اَللَّهُمَّ هَـٰذِهِ نَاصِيَتِيْ ، فَتَقَبَّلْ مِنِّيْ ،
وَاغْفِرْلِيْ ذُنُوْبِيْ ، اَللَّهُمَّ اغْفِرْ لِيْ وَلِلْمُحَلِّقِيْنَ وَالْـمُقَصِّرِيْنَ ،
يَا وَاسِعَ الْـمَغْفِرَةِ. آمِيْن.

In the name of Allah, the All-Merciful, the Compassionate. O Allah, this is my forelock, so accept from me and forgive my sins. O Allah, forgive me, those who shave their heads and those who shorten their hair, O Immense Forgiver. Āmīn.

When one has finished, bury the hair and recite,

أَلْحَمْدُ لله الَّذِيْ قَضَى عَنَّا نُسُكَنَا ، اَللَّهُمَّ زِدْنَا إِيْمَـانًا وَيَقِيْنًا ،
وَتَوْفِيْقًا وَعَوْنًا ، وَاغْفِرْ لَنَا وَلِآبَائِنَا وَأُمَّهَاتِنَا وَالْـمُسْلِمِيْنَ أَجْمَعِيْنَ.

119 According to the Shāfi'īs it is three hairs, while according to the Mālikīs it is to completely shave one's head or shorten the hair, which is more prudent for one, regardless of which school of law one adheres to, in emulation of the Prophet ﷺ, because he shaved his head completely and said, 'Learn from me your rites.'

All praise belongs to Allah, who has accomplished for us our rites. O Allah, increase us in faith and certainty, in success and assistance, and forgive us, our fathers, our mothers and all Muslims.

THE *ṬAWĀF* OF THE VISIT (*ṬAWĀF AL-ZIYĀRAH*) [ALSO KNOWN AS THE *ṬAWĀF* OF DEPARTURE (*ṬAWĀF AL-IFĀḌAH*)]

When one has finished having the head shaved, leave for Mecca to perform the *Ṭawāf* of the Visit *(Ṭawāf al-Ziyārah)*, which is an integral of hajj by the consensus of Muslims. So circumambulate the House seven times. If one performed the *saʿy* prior to the standing in ʿArafah, then the *saʿy* is no longer necessary, nor is it sunnah for one to briskly strut or bare the right shoulder and cover the left during this *ṭawāf*. If one has not previously performed the *saʿy*, then it is now necessary for one to perform it after this *ṭawāf*, in which case it is a sunnah for one to bare the right shoulder and cover the left during the entire *ṭawāf*, while briskly strutting in the first three cycles only.

As for someone performing hajj and umrah simultaneously (*qārin*), then he needs to perform another *saʿy* if he had only performed one upon arrival. However, if one had performed two *ṭawāf*s and two *saʿy*s upon arrival, then another *saʿy* is no longer necessary.[120]

Perform the *Ṭawāf* of the Visit (*Ṭawāf al-Ziyārah*) in the same manner as the *Ṭawāf of* Arrival (*Ṭawāf al-Qudūm*) and

---

120 According to the Shāfiʿīs, Mālikīs and Ḥanbalīs, a single *ṭawāf* and *saʿy* suffice one, as in the case of a *mufrid*.

be vigilant in observing its internal meanings, and observe here the notion of gaining acceptance and honour, just as a visitor is honoured by the host, for one is here a visitor of 'the Real' [Allah], Transcendent and Exalted, and He is the most generous of hosts. This is demonstrated by the authentic noble hadith: 'Those performing hajj and umrah are Allah's visitors; if they supplicate to Him, He answers them, and if they seek His forgiveness, He forgives them.'

The first release from iḥrām (al-taḥallul al-awwal)

After the first release, also called the lesser release, all things unlawful during *iḥrām* become lawful, with the exception of [sexual contact with] one's wife. The first release occurs upon shaving one's head.[121]

The second release from iḥrām (al-taḥallul al-thānī)

It is also called the greater release, and it occurs after the performance of the *Ṭawāf* of Departure if it is preceded by the shaving of one's head.[122]

---

121 According to the Shāfiʿīs and Ḥanbalīs, the lesser release occurs by doing two of three things: stoning, shaving and the *Ṭawāf* of the Visit (which is preceded by the *saʿy*; otherwise, one is not released, except by performing the *saʿy* after the *Ṭawāf* of the Visit) in relation to someone performing hajj only (*mufrid*), and likewise someone performing hajj and umrah simultaneously (*qārin*) or individually (*mutamattiʿ*). Imam Mālik is of the opinion that the first release only occurs by throwing the stones at the site of ʿAqabah.

122 According to the Shāfiʿīs and Ḥanbalīs this release occurs by doing the third of the three things: stoning, shaving and the *Ṭawāf* of the Visit (if preceded by the *saʿy*); otherwise, according to them, one is not released until one performs the *saʿy*. According to the Mālikīs the greater release occurs upon performing the *Ṭawāf* of Departure

The first and second days of al-Tashrīq *(the second and third days of Eid)*

It is better, if feasible for one, to hasten in returning to Minā immediately after the *Ṭawāf* of the Visit (*Ṭawāf al-Ziyārah*) in order to reach there for the noon prayer, in emulation of the Prophetic Sunnah and that one may undertake the rituals of these two days, which are:

1. spending the nights of these two days in Minā, which is a sunnah;[123]
2. and stoning the three sites.

It is necessary for one to stone all three sites on these two days, and these are [in order]:

1. the smaller site *(al-Jamrah al-Sughrā*) or [also called] the first [site], which is the one immediately after the Khayf Mosque (*Masjid al-Khayf*);
2. the intermediate site (*al-Jamrah al-Wusṭā*) or [also called] the second;
3. and the greater site (*al-Jamrah al-Kubrā*), which is the ʿAqabah site (*Jamrah al-ʿAqabah*), and it is the furthest of the sites from the Khayf Mosque.

The time for the stoning begins when the sun moves away from the zenith on the first day of *al-Tashrīq*, namely the second day of Eid, by the consensus of the scholars. So

---

[*Ṭawāf* of the Visit] for whoever has shaved the head and stoned the site of ʿAqabah before the *Ṭawāf* of Departure, or its [stoning the site of ʿAqabah's] time has elapsed, on the condition that the *saʿy* has also been previously performed.

123 According to the other schools, it is necessary.

begin with the smaller site ('the first'), the site closest to the Khayf Mosque: throw seven stones at it from whichever direction, reciting with every throw,

بِسْمِ اللهِ وَاللهُ أَكْبَرُ، رَغْماً لِلشَّيْطَانِ وَحِزْبِهِ ، وَرِضاً لِلرَّحْمَـٰنِ.

In the name of Allah, and Allah is the greatest, in humiliation of Satan and his party, and in seeking pleasure from the All-Merciful.

When one has finished, step aside and face the qiblah, and turn to Allah, supplicating and reciting the invocations and the Qur'an, in emulation of the Prophetic Sunnah, because of the Prophet's words ﷺ, 'The stoning of the sites and the *sa'y* between al-Ṣafā and al-Marwah were only prescribed to establish the remembrance of Allah.'

This is one of the occasions wherein one's prayers are expected to be answered, and it is recommended to prolong one's standing for the duration it takes to recite a thirtieth portion (*juz'*) of the Qur'an. One can supplicate with whatever of the previous supplications in the *ṭawāf, sa'y* and standing [in 'Arafah, which have been mentioned earlier], as they are suitable for all occasions; therefore, supplicate with whatever one desires.

Then stone the intermediate site ('the second'), also pausing after stoning it, just as one did after the first in terms of prolongation and supplication. Thereafter, head towards the 'Aqabah site ('the greater site' or 'the third'), and throw seven stones at it also, but instead of pausing after stoning it, head towards wherever one wishes.

The time for the stoning lasts till dawn of the following day, though it is offensive after sunset. Thus if one postpones it till dawn, it will become necessary for one to offer a sacrifice according to the Ḥanafīs.[124]

When it is noon (*zawāl*) on the following day, stone the three sites as one did the previous day. The time for stoning on this day, like the previous day, begins from *zawāl*[125] and ends at dawn break.[126]

Stay in Minā throughout that period, spending the nights therein, and profusely recite the Qur'an, and invoke and supplicate to Allah. Be eager to perform the prayer at the Khayf Mosque in Minā and maintain fear of Allah throughout, as one enters and exits Minā, as these days of Minā are days of remembrance and worship.

THE FIRST DEPARTURE (*AL-NAFR AL-AWWAL*)

When one has stoned the sites on the second day of *Tashrīq*, then it is permissible for one to leave for Mecca, and one is exempt from the stoning on the third day as long as one passes the borders of Minā before dawn break.[127] This is

---

124 It is also necessary for one to sacrifice according to the Mālikīs if one postpones it till sunset; so one would have to make it up and expiate by slaughtering. According to the Shāfi'īs and Ḥanbalīs, the time lasts till sunset on the fourth day.

125 A contrary narration from Abu Ḥanīfah states that if one wants to depart during the second day of *Tashrīq*, then it is permissible for one to stone the sites before noon (*ẓuhr*). The fatwa is issued according to this narration out of necessity and due to severe congestion; however, postponing the stoning until the fourth day is much more preferable, and there is in that the revival of the Sunnah.

126 And at sunset according to the Mālikīs, whereas according to the Shāfi'īs and Ḥanbalīs it lasts till sunset on the fourth day.

127 And before sunset according to the Shāfi'īs.

called the first departure. If one does not leave Minā by dawn break, then one is to remain behind in Minā, as it has become necessary for one to stone [the sites] on the third day of *Tashrīq*.

It is recommended during one's departure to Mecca, and in the rest of one's travels, to recite the invocations recommended for travellers, such as invoking the *takbīr* [Allah is the greatest (*Allāhu akbar*)], *tahlīl* [There is no deity except Allah (*Lā ilāha illa llāh*)], glorifying Allah (*tamjīd*), invoking blessings upon the Prophet ﷺ, reciting the Qur'an and pleading for acceptance, facilitation and so forth.

Amongst the supplications which have been transmitted from the scholars during the departure is the following:

أَلْحَمْدُ لِلّٰهِ حَمْداً كَثِيْراً طَيِّباً مُبَارَكاً فِيْهِ ، والشُّكْرُ لَهُ عَلَى أَدَاءِ الْـمَنَاسِكِ وَالتَّوْفِيْقِ لِأَدَاءِ الْحَجِّ إِلَى بَيْتِ اللهِ ، وَتَيْسِيْرِ ذَلِكَ بِمَنِّهِ وَكَرَمِهِ ، اَللَّهُمَّ فَتَقَبَّلْ مِنَّا الْحَجَّ وَأَثِبْنَا عَلَيْهِ ، وَاجْعَلْهُ لَنَا خَالِصاً لِوَجْهِكَ الْكَرِيْمِ ، وَانْفَعْنَا بِهِ يَوْمَ لَا يَنْفَعُ مَالٌ وَلَا بَنُوْنَ إِلَّا مَنْ أَتَى اللهَ بِقَلْبٍ سَلِيْمٍ.

Praise belongs to Allah, an abundant, pure and blessed praise, and thanks are due to Him for enabling us to perform the rites and giving success in performing the pilgrimage to Allah's house, and facilitating that out of His favour and generosity. O Allah, so accept this hajj from us and reward us for it, make it for us sincerely for Your noble countenance, and benefit us by it on that day wherein wealth and children will be of no use, except someone who comes to Allah with a pure heart.

The third day of al-Tashrīq *(the fourth day of Eid)*

It is necessary for whoever has stayed behind till this day, and did not leave during the first departure, to stone the three sites. Staying behind for this day is better than hastily leaving before it by the consensus of the scholars; so be eager to do so in order to revive the Sunnah.

The time for this session of stoning begins after dawn and ends at sunset.[128] Similarly, the time for stoning [the sites] for the previous days expires at sunset on this day, as does its make up [*qaḍā*] time; thus it is necessary for one to expiate by the consensus of the Imams [if it is missed].

THE SECOND DEPARTURE (*AL-NAFR AL-THĀNĪ*)

With this session of stoning, the rites of Minā are concluded, and the pilgrims all leave for Mecca, having achieved their hearts' desire. This is called 'the second departure', and it is not legitimate to stay behind in Minā after the stoning on this day.

The supplication for the second departure is the same as the one mentioned above for the first departure.

Furthermore, if one stays in Mecca, then know that one is a neighbour to Allah's House, so give the neighbour His due in terms of etiquette and presence of heart, and adhere to performing the prayers in the *Ḥaram* [the Sacred Mosque] and profusely performing *ṭawāf*. If one becomes tired, then sit down to behold the House, because mercy descends upon those who gaze at Allah's House.

128 And after *zawāl* according to the other three Imams.

The umrah of someone performing hajj only (mufrid)

If one has performed hajj only, then perform an umrah: go out to the region of *al-Ḥill* so that one may enter the *iḥrām* for umrah from it. The closest region in *al-Ḥill* to Mecca is al-Tanʿīm, which is the place that people in Mecca go to for entering the *iḥrām* for umrah; and the place is known by the name 'the Mosques of 'Ā'ishah' because the Prophet ﷺ sent 'Ā'ishah to al-Tanʿīm, whereby she entered the *iḥrām* for umrah.

The method of performing the rites for umrah has already been explained, so perform it accordingly.

The Farewell Ṭawāf (Ṭawāf al-Wadāʿ)

When one wishes to travel [and leave Mecca], circumambulate the House without briskly strutting, baring the right shoulder and covering the left (*iḍṭibāʿ*) and performing the *saʿy* after it. This is called the Farewell *Ṭawāf* (*Ṭawāf al-Wadāʿ*), and it is necessary. Its allocated time is after the *Ṭawāf* of the Visit; thus any *ṭawāf* performed thereafter will account for the Farewell *Ṭawāf*, even if one delays travelling after it by days and nights.[129]

If a woman is menstruating or in her lochia, then she is exempt from the Farewell *Ṭawāf*, though it is recommended for her to stand at the door of the *Ḥaram* [the Sacred Mosque] and supplicate.

The thought that one should observe in this *ṭawāf* is for concluding one's hajj to Allah's inviolable House, for

---

129 According to other than the Ḥanafīs, it is necessary for one to perform it just before travelling.

a guest does not depart except after seeking permission from the host; and it is from the custom of kings, nobles and dignitaries that whoever returns home after their hospitality should return with a prize and an award. The pilgrims are Allah's visitors and guests; so whoever returns from Allah's house should at least return back forgiven. So perceive these meanings during the Farewell *Ṭawāf* and supplicate with those supplications of *ṭawāf* which one knows, followed by performing the two cycles of prayer for *ṭawāf*, as explained earlier.

Thereafter, go to the Zamzam well and drink from its water,[130] facing the House [Kaaba] and drinking to one's fill. Continuously gaze at the House as one drinks, pour some Zamzam over one's body and wipe one's face and head with it. When drinking the water, intend whatever one wishes, because Zamzam is for whatever intention accompanies the drinking.

Then approach the Kaaba and hold onto the Multazam, beseeching Allah Most High, supplicating for the things one loves of this world and the next, beginning by praising and extolling Allah, invoking blessings and peace upon the noble Prophet ﷺ and concluding it with such a formula. Within the supplication try and recite the following:

اَللَّهُمَّ الْبَيْتُ بَيْتُكَ ، وَالْعَبْدُ عَبْدُكَ وَابْنُ عَبْدِكَ ، وَابْنُ أَمَتِكَ ،
حَمَلْتَنِي عَلَى مَا سَخَّرْتَ لِيْ مِنْ خَلْقِكَ ، وَبَلَّغْتَنِي بِنِعْمَتِكَ حَتَّى

130 [T] It is no longer feasible to drink from the well itself as there is no access to it, but one should, nevertheless, drink Zamzam water in emulation of the Sunnah.

أَعَنْتَنِي عَلَى قَضَاءِ مَنَاسِكِكَ ، فَإِنْ كُنْتَ رَضِيْتَ عَنِّيْ فَزِدْنِيْ
مِنْكَ رِضاً ، وَإِلَّا فَمُنَّ عَلَيَّ بِالْقَبُوْلِ وَالرِّضَا مِنْ مَحْضِ فَضْلِكَ ،
يَا ذَا الْفَضْلِ الْعَظِيْمِ ، هَا أَنَا مُنْصَرِفٌ بِإِذْنِكَ ، غَيْرَ مُسْتَبْدِلٍ
بِكَ وَلَا بَيْتِكَ ، وَلَا رَاغِبٍ عَنْكَ وَلَا عَنْ بَيْتِكَ.

O Allah, the House is Your House, and the slave is Your slave, the son of Your slave and the son of Your bondswoman. You have driven me on that which You have subdued for me of Your creation and have enabled me to reach [the destination] by Your favour until You assisted me in accomplishing Your rites. So if You are satisfied with me, increase Your satisfaction with me; otherwise, favour me with acceptance and satisfaction out of Your pure grace, O Possessor of immense grace. Here I am, leaving by Your permission, not exchanging for You or Your house [for anything else], nor out of aversion to You or Your house.

اَللَّهُمَّ فاصْحَبْنِيَ الْعَافِيَةَ فِيْ بَدَنِيْ وَالْعِصْمَةَ فِيْ دِيْنِي ، وَأَحْسِنْ
مُنْقَلَبِي ، وَارْزُقْنِي طَاعَتَكَ مَا أَبقَيْتَنِيْ ، وَاجْمَعْ لِيْ خَيْرَيِ
الْآخِرَةِ وَالدُّنْيَا ، إِنَّكَ عَلَى كُلِّ شَيْءٍ قَدِيْرٌ.

O Allah, let well-being accompany me in my body and protection in my religion; make my return well, enable me to obey You as long as You keep me alive, and gather for me the best of the next world and this world. Verily, You have power over everything.

اَللّٰهُمَّ ارْزُقْنِيَ الْعَوْدَ بَعْدَ الْعَوْدِ ، أَلْـمَرَّةَ بَعْدَ الْـمَرَّةِ ، إِلَى بَيْتِكَ الْحَرَامِ ، وَاجْعَلْنِي مِنَ الْـمَقْبُوْلِيْنَ عِنْدَكَ ، يَا ذَا الْجَلَالِ وَالْإِكْرَامِ، اَللّٰهُمَّ لَا تَجْعَلْهُ آخِرَ الْعَهْدِ مِنْ بَيْتِكَ الْحَرَامِ ، يَا أَرْحَمَ الرَّاحِمِيْنَ.

O Allah, allow me to continuously return, time after time, to Your Inviolable House, and make me from amongst those who are accepted by You, O Possessor of majesty and generosity. O Allah, do not let it be the last visit to Your Inviolable House, O Most Merciful of the Merciful.

Then touch and kiss the Black Stone, or point to it if one encounters congestion, and walk towards the door of the Ḥaram with one's face towards the door, and do not walk backwards, for the scholars have considered that offensive. Moreover, repeatedly turn towards the revered Kaaba, out of grief in parting from it, such that one leaves with one's heart certain of being pardoned and forgiven, having achieved success and Allah's satisfaction. Depart with one's heart attached to the House, because whoever's heart is attached to a mosque, Allah will shade him under the shade of His throne on that day when there will be no shade except His shade. So whoever's heart is attached to the Ancient House, then it is befitting that he will succeed with safety and tranquillity under the shade of the throne of the All-Merciful.

5

Visiting the Prophet ﷺ

Allah has distinguished this nation in that the resting place of its Prophet ﷺ is known with certainty, and in that there is a remedy for the hearts from bewilderment, since tranquillity settles within them out of their burning desire [for him]. Muslims have consistently, from the time of the early righteous Muslim generations ﵃, visited him ﷺ and expended much effort to travel to him, because it is from amongst the most important lofty goals and beneficial devotional acts accepted by Allah Most High.

When one wishes to visit him ﷺ, one should intend to visit his noble mosque also, so that the sunnah of visiting the mosque and its reward is gained, as it is one of the three mosques to which one is to undertake travel. Abū Hurayrah ﵁ relates that the Messenger of Allah ﷺ said, 'Luggage is not tied [an expression for preparation for a journey] except to three mosques: this mosque of mine [in Medina], al-Ḥaram Mosque [in Mecca] and al-Aqṣā Mosque [in Jerusalem].' (It is an agreed upon narration.)

When one beholds the date orchards of Medina, invoke blessings upon him ﷺ and recite,

اَللَّهُمَّ هَـٰذَا حَرَمُ نَبِيِّكَ فَاجْعَلْهُ وِقَايَةً لِيْ مِنَ النَّارِ
وَأَمَانًا مِنَ الْعَذَابِ وَسُوْءِ الْحِسَابِ.

O Allah, this is the Sacred Precinct of Your Prophet, so make it a protection for me from the Fire and a security from punishment and a bad reckoning.

It is recommended for one to bathe when one enters the Illuminated Medina, wear one's cleanest clothes and internalise in one's heart the nobility of Medina and that the one ﷺ by whom it was honoured is the best of creation. Maintain the sense of reverence from the beginning of one's arrival until one departs, with one's heart full of awe, and profusely invoke blessings and salutations upon him ﷺ.

The manner of visiting him ﷺ

When one arrives at the door of the Prophetic Mosque, enter reciting the well-known invocation for entering mosques,

اَللَّهُمَّ صَلِّ عَلَى سَيِّدِنَا مُحَمَّدٍ وَعَلَى آلِهِ وَسَلِّمْ، رَبِّ اغْفِرْ
لِيْ ذُنُوْبِيْ وَافْتَحْ لِيْ أَبْوَابَ رَحْمَتِكَ.

O Allah, send your reverential mercy on our master Muhammad and his family and give them peace. My Lord, forgive me my sins and open for me the doors to Your mercy.

Upon leaving the mosque one uses the beginning part of the same supplication, but with the wording,

وَافْتَحْ لِيْ أَبْوابَ فَضْلِكَ.

And open for me the doors to Your bounty.

Firstly, perform two units of prayer as a greeting to the mosque, and then proceed towards the noble chamber wherein is his tomb ﷺ. One then turns one's back towards the qiblah and faces the noble tomb. Stand in front of the left round window at a distance of four-arm's length in veneration and respect for the Chosen One ﷺ, with one's heart devoid of worldly attachments, reflecting on the grandeur of one's location, and the rank of the one in whose presence one stands, because one is here before the face of the Messenger of Allah ﷺ; so greet him without raising your voice and say,

أَلسَّلَامُ عَلَيْكَ يَا رَسُوْلَ اللهِ ، أَلسَّلَامُ عَلَيْكَ يَا نَبِيَّ اللهِ ، أَلسَّلَامُ عَلَيْكَ يَا صَفِيَّ اللهِ ، أَلسَّلَامُ عَلَيْكَ يَا نَبِيَّ الرَّحْمَةِ ، أَلسَّلَامُ عَلَيْكَ يَا خَاتَمَ النَّبِيِّيْنَ ، أَلسَّلَامُ عَلَيْكَ يَا مُزَّمِّلُ ، أَلسَّلَامُ عَلَيْكَ يَا مُدَّثِّرُ ، أَلسَّلَامُ عَلَيْكَ يا مُحَمَّدُ ، أَلسَّلَامُ عَلَيْكَ يَا أَيُّهَا النَّبِيُّ أَحْمَدُ ، أَلسَّلَامُ عَلَيْكَ وَعَلى أَهْلِ بَيْتِكَ الطَّيِّبِيْنَ الطَّاهِرِيْنَ الَّذِيْنَ أَذْهَبَ اللهُ عَنْهُمُ الرِّجْسَ وَطَهَّرَهُمْ تَطْهِيْراً. جَزَاكَ اللهُ عَنَّا أَفْضَلَ مَا جَزَى نَبِيّاً عَنْ قَوْمِهِ ، وَرَسُوْلاً عَنْ أُمَّتِهِ ، أَشْهَدُ أَنْ لَا إِلَـٰهَ إِلَّا اللهُ وَأَنَّكَ رَسُوْلُ اللهِ ، قَدْ بَلَّغْتَ الرِّسَالَةَ وَأَدَّيْتَ الْأَمَانَةَ ، وَأَوْضَحْتَ الْحُجَّةَ وَجَاهَدْتَ فِي اللهِ حَقَّ جِهَادِهِ.

Peace be upon you, O the Messenger of Allah. Peace be upon you, O Prophet of Allah. Peace be upon you, O Allah's chosen one. Peace be upon you, O Prophet of Mercy. Peace be upon you, O Seal of the Prophets. Peace be upon you,

O Enwrapped one. Peace be upon you, O Shrouded one. Peace be upon you, O Muhammad. Peace be upon you, O Prophet Aḥmad. Peace be upon you and upon the pure good members of your household, from whom Allah removed impurities and purified. May Allah reward you on our behalf the best of what He rewarded a prophet on behalf of his nation and a messenger on behalf of his community. I bear witness that there is no deity except Allah and that you are the Messenger of Allah. You have conveyed the message, discharged the trust, clarified the proof and truly struggled for the sake of Allah.

اَللَّهُمَّ آتِ سَيِّدِنَا مُحَمَّداً الْوَسِيْلَةَ وَالْفَضِيْلَةَ وَابْعَثْهُ مَقَاماً مَحْمُوْداً الَّذِيْ وَعَدْتَهُ ، وَآتِهِ نِهَايَةَ مَا يَنْبَغِيْ أَنْ يَسْأَلُهُ السَّائِلُونَ ، اَللَّهُمَّ صَلِّ عَلَى سَيِّدِنَا مُحَمَّدٍ عَبْدِكَ وَرَسُوْلِكَ ، أَلنَّبِيِّ الْأُمِّيِّ وَعَلَى آلِ مُحَمَّدٍ وَأَزْوَاجِهِ وَذُرِّيَّتِهِ ، كَمَا صَلَّيْتَ عَلَى إِبْرَاهِيْمَ وَعَلَى آلِ إِبْرَاهِيْمَ ، وَبَارِكْ عَلَى مُحَمَّدٍ وَعَلَى آلِ مُحَمَّدٍ ، كَمَا بَارَكْتَ عَلَى إِبْرَاهِيْمَ وَعَلَى آلِ إِبْرَاهِيْمَ ،
فِي الْعَالَمِيْنَ إِنَّكَ حَمِيْدٌ مَجِيْدٌ.

O Allah, give our master Muhammad the wasīlah and the privilege,[131] *and raise him to a praiseworthy rank that you have promised him, and give him the pinnacle of what people should ask him. O Allah, send your reverential mercy upon our master Muhammad, your servant and messenger, the Unlettered Prophet, and the family of Muhammad and his wives and offspring, just as You sent Your reverential*

131 [T] The *wasīlah* has been interpreted as a lofty rank in Paradise or intercession for the believers on the Day of Resurrection.

*mercy upon our master Ibrāhīm and the family
of Ibrāhīm, and bless Muhammad and the family of
Muhammad just as you have blessed Ibrāhīm and the
family of Ibrāhīm within all of the worlds. Verily,
You are the praised, the majestic.*

If anyone has requested you to convey his greetings to him ﷺ, say, 'Peace be upon you, O Messenger of Allah from So-and-so, the son of So-and-so,' or 'So-and-so, the son of So-and-so, conveys his greetings to you, O Messenger of Allah,' or the like.

Thereafter, supplicate for whatever good one wishes for oneself, for those whom one loves, for those who have requested one's prayers and for all the Muslims.

Then step back an arm span towards the right to greet *al-Ṣiddīq al-Akbar*, our master Abū Bakr ؓ, because his head is at the shoulder of the Messenger of Allah ﷺ,[132] and say,

أَلسَّلَامُ عَلَيْكَ يَا خَلِيْفَةَ رَسُوْلِ الله، أَلسَّلَامُ عَلَيْكَ يَا صَاحِبَ رَسُوْلِ الله فِي الْغَارِ، أَلسَّلَامُ عَلَيْكَ يَا رَفِيْقَهُ فِي الْأَسْفَارِ، أَلسَّلَامُ عَلَيْكَ يَا أَمِيْنَهُ عَلَى الْأَسْرَارِ، جَزَاكَ اللهُ عَنَّا أَفْضَلَ مَا جَزَى إِمَاماً عَنْ أُمَّةِ نَبِيِّهِ، لَقَدْ خَلَفْتَهُ بِأَحْسَنِ خِلْفَةٍ، وَسَلَكْتَ طَرِيْقَهُ وَمِنْهَاجَهُ خَيْرَ مَسْلَكٍ، وَقَاتَلْتَ أَهْلَ الرِّدَّةِ وَالْبِدَعِ، وَمَهَّدْتَ الْإِسْلَامَ، وَوَصَلْتَ الْأَرْحَامَ، وَلَمْ تَزَلْ قَائِماً بِالْحَقِّ نَاصِراً لِأَهْلِهِ حَتَّى أَتَاكَ الْيَقِيْنُ، فَالسَّلَامُ عَلَيْكَ وَرَحْمَةُ اللهِ وَبَرَكَاتُهُ.

---

132 [T] This is if one is approaching the blessed grave from the Baqīʿ gate, i.e. from the direction of his blessed feet.

Peace be upon you, O Successor of Allah's Messenger. Peace be upon you, O Companion of Allah's Messenger in the cave. Peace be upon you, O Companion of his during travel. Peace be upon you, O Trustee of his over his secrets. May Allah reward you on our behalf the best of what He rewarded an imam on behalf of his prophet's community. You succeeded him in the best manner, and you followed his path and way in the best manner, and you fought those who apostatised and introduced blamewor thy innovations, and you paved the way for Islam. You maintained the ties of kinship, you continued to stand for the truth, supporting its propagators until death [literally certainty] came to you; so may Allah's peace, mercy and blessings be upon you.

Then step a [further] arm's span towards the right to 'al-Fārūq', the one through whom Allah reinforced Islam, our master 'Umar ibn al-Khaṭṭāb ﵁, and say,

أَلسَّلَامُ عَلَيْكَ يَا أَمِيْرَ الْمُؤْمِنِيْنَ ، أَلسَّلَامُ عَلَيْكَ يَا مُظْهِرَ الْإِسْلَامِ،
أَلسَّلَامُ عَلَيْكَ يَا مُكَسِّرَ الْأَصْنَامِ ، جَزاكَ اللهُ عَنَّا أَفْضَلَ الْجَزَاءِ ،
وَرَضِيَ عَمَّنْ اسْتَخْلَفَكَ ، فَلَقَدْ نَصَرْتَ الْإِسْلَامَ وَالْـمُسْلِمِيْنَ وَ كَفَلْتَ
الْأَيْتَامَ وَ وَصَلْتَ الْأَرْحَامَ وَ قَوِيَ بِكَ الْإِسْـلَامُ ، وَكُنْتَ لِلْمُسْلِمِيْنَ
إِمَاماً مَرْضِـيّاً ، وَهَادِياً مَهْدِيّاً ، جَمَعْتَ شَـمْلَهُمْ ، وَأَغْنَيْتَ فَقِيْرَهُمْ ،
وَأَجْبَرْتَ كَسْرَهُمْ ، فَالسَّلَامُ عَلَيْكَ وَرَحْمَةُ اللهِ وَبَرَكاتُهُ.

Peace be upon you, O Leader of the Believers. Peace be upon you, O Propagator of Islam. Peace be upon you, O Breaker of Idols. May Allah reward you on our behalf

the best of reward and satisfaction for those who succeeded you, for you supported Islam and Muslims: you took care of orphans, maintained the ties of kinship, and through you Islam was reinforced, and you were for the Muslims an Imam with whom they were pleased and a rightly guided guide; you united them, enriched their poor, mended their broken hearts; so may Allah's peace, mercy and blessings be upon you.

An important point for the visitor regarding the etiquette of his visit

The jurists of the relied upon Islamic schools of law have ruled on the offensiveness of rubbing oneself against the Prophet's tomb ﷺ or the metal grid of his chamber. These are the words of Imam al-Nawawī on the subject,

> It is not permissible to circumambulate his tomb ﷺ, and it is offensive to touch the wall of the grave with one's back or stomach. They have said that it is offensive to wipe it [the grave] with one's hand and kiss it; rather, the proper etiquette is that one stands away from him just as one would have done in his presence during his lifetime ﷺ. This is what is correct, which the scholars have stated and upon which they have concurred, and let no one be deceived by the contrary practice of many laymen, because emulation and action is only in accordance with authentic hadiths and the opinions of the scholars, and one should ignore the innovations and ignorant practices of laymen and others.

The Sacred Precinct (*Ḥaram*) of Medina and the etiquette of staying therein

Know that Medina is similar to Mecca in virtue and sanctity, so during one's stay in Medina one should maintain a sense of its grandeur in one's heart and that it is the city which Allah chose for His Prophet ﷺ to migrate to and in which to settle, be buried in and where revelation was to descend upon him. Recollect his frequent movements therein ﷺ: his walking in its quarters and its other virtues.

Furthermore, one should, during the stay, perform all prayers in the Prophetic Mosque and intend retreat therein just as in all other mosques. Abū Hurayrah رضي الله عنه relates that the Prophet ﷺ said, 'A prayer in this mosque of mine is better than a thousand prayers elsewhere, except the Sacred Mosque [in Mecca],' and it is an agreed-upon narration. Endeavour to pray in the Rawḍah [literally the garden], which is between his grave and pulpit ﷺ, designated by the white pillars. It has been related from ʿAbd-Allah ibn Zayd رضي الله عنه (in an agreed-upon narration) that the Messenger of Allah ﷺ said, 'One of the gardens of Paradise is situated between my house and my pulpit;' and his grave ﷺ is in his house.

It is recommended that one should fast as much as possible during one's stay in Medina, and that one give in charity to the Messenger of Allah's neighbours ﷺ, and they are the residents of Medina: its natives or migrants.

Visiting the historical sites

It is recommended that one visit the historical sites in Medina, which are about thirty places and known by the residents of Medina. The following are the well-known sites for visiting:

1. al-Baqīʿ: it is recommended that one frequent al-Baqīʿ, especially on Saturday. When one enters it, say,

أَلسَّلَامُ عَلَيْكُمْ دَارَ قَوْمٍ مُؤْمِنِيْنَ ، وَإِنَّا إِنْ شَاءَ اللهُ بِكُمْ لَاحِقُوْنَ ، اَللَّهُمَّ اغْفِرْ لِأَهْلِ بَقِيْعِ الْغَرْقَدِ ، اَللَّهُمَّ اغْفِرْ لَنَا وَلَهُمْ.

Peace be upon you, abode of believers, and we, if Allah wills, will join you. O Allah, forgive the people of of Baqīʿal-Gharqad. Allah, forgive us and them.

Whenever convenient, visit the graves of the great ones in al-Baqī ʿ, such as the graves of Ibrāhīm (the Messenger of Allah's son ﷺ), ʿUthmān, al-ʿAbbās, Ṣafiyyah the Messenger's paternal aunt ﷺ, al-Ḥasan ibn ʿAlī, Jaʿfar ibn Muḥammad and others ﵃. Greet each one of them individually and pray that they receive the best [reward] and lofty ranks;

2. the Martyrs of Uḥud. It is recommended for one to visit the graves of the Martyrs on any day; however, it is best on Thursday. Upon arrival at the site, one begins with Hamzah, the paternal uncle of the Prophet ﷺ, the leader of the martyrs ﵁. Greet them all and pray for them with the transmitted supplication that is read in the funeral prayer, since the Prophet ﷺ prayed for them with it at the end of his life, and say,

سَلَامٌ عَلَيْكُمْ بِمَا صَبَرْتُمْ فَنِعْمَ عُقْبَى الدَّارِ.

Peace be upon you for the patience that you endured, for what a wonderful final abode it is [that is promised for you];

3. the Qubā' Mosque. It is the first mosque to be established in Islam, and the first person to place a stone in it was the Messenger of Allah ﷺ. It is emphatically recommended for one to go to the Qubā' Mosque, and it is more emphasised on Saturday, in emulation of Prophet ﷺ. In going there, one should intend to draw near to Allah by visiting and praying therein. It has been related from Usayd ibn Ẓuhayr that the Messenger of Allah ﷺ said, 'A prayer in the Qubā' Mosque is like an umrah.' Al-Tirmidhī related it and said, 'This hadith is authentic, solitary.'

Amongst the supplications read in this mosque which the scholars have mentioned is:

يَا صَرِيْخَ الْـمُسْتَصْرِخِيْنَ، وَ يَا مُفَرِّجَ كَرْبِ الْـمَكْرُوْبِيْنَ، يَا غِيَاثَ
الْـمُسْتَغِيْثِيْنَ، يَا مُجِيْبَ دَعْوَةِ الْـمُضْطَرِّيْنَ، صَلِّ اللّٰهُمَّ عَلَى مُحَمَّدٍ
وَآلِهِ وَسَلِّمْ تَسْلِيْماً ، وَاكْشِفْ كَرْبِيْ وَحُزْنِيْ كَمَا كَشَفْتَ عَنْ
رَسُوْلِ اللهِ ﷺ حُزْنَهُ وَكَرْبَهُ فِيْ هَـٰذَا الْـمَقَامِ ، يَا حَنَّانُ يَا مَنَّانُ ،
يَا كَثِيْرَ الْـمَعْرُوْفِ ، يَا دَائِمَ الْإِحْسَانِ ، يَا أَرْحَمَ الرَّاحِمِيْنَ.

O the One to whom people cry for help, the aid of those who seek aid, the reliever of the distressed, the answerer of the call of those in dire need, send Your reverential mercy, O Allah, upon Muhammad and his family and give them peace, and remove my distress and sorrow, just as you removed them from the Messenger of Allah ﷺ in this place [maqām], O Compassionate One, the One Who bestows favours, the Profusely Generous One, the Eternally Kind and the Most Merciful of the Merciful.

Bidding farewell to Medina

When one has decided to return to one's family, it is recommended that one bid farewell to the mosque by performing two units of prayer therein, supplicating after them for whatever one desires. Then approach the noble presence and greet the Messenger of Allah ﷺ and his two companions as described earlier, and pray for whatever one wants, for oneself, one's parents, one's children and one's brothers and sisters, while being remorseful, regretful, weeping and sad. Also, ask Allah for a return to one's family, safely, successfully and with protection from the tribulations of this world and the next.

Ask Allah that He does not make this the final encounter [with these holy lands] and say,

اَللّٰهُمَّ لَا تَجْعَلْهُ آخِرَ الْعَهْدِ بِحَرَمِ رَسُوْلِكَ ، وَسَهِّلْ لِيَ الْعَوْدَ
إِلَى الْحَرَمَيْنِ سَبِيْلاً سَهْلَةً ، وَارْزُقْنِيَ الْعَفْوَ وَالْعَافِيَةَ فِي
الْآخِرَةِ وَالدُّنْيَا ، وَرُدَّنَا إِلَيْهِ سَالِمِيْنَ غَانِمِيْنَ.

O Allah, do not make it the last encounter with the Sacred Precinct of your Messenger, facilitate for me to return to the two Sacred Precincts, grant me pardon and protection in the next world and in this world and return us to him safely and successfully.

Then depart, weeping and regretful for parting from the noble prophetic presence [*haḍrah*].

It is a sunnah for the traveller when returning home to chant the *takbīr* [invoke Allah is the greatest] on every place high off the ground, and to recite the supplication for travelling which was mentioned earlier from the hadith, which is,

سُبْحَانَ الَّذِيْ سَخَّرَ لَنَا هَـٰذَا

Glory be to the One who has subjugated for us this ...,

and one adds to it the words which have been related from the Prophet ﷺ when returning,

آيِبُوْنَ ، تَائِبُوْنَ ، عَابِدُوْنَ ، سَاجِدُوْنَ ، لِرَبِّنَا حَامِدُوْنَ ، صَدَقَ اللهُ وَعْدَهُ ، وَنَصَرَ عَبْدَهُ ، وَهَزَمَ الْأَحْزَابَ وَحْدَهُ.

Returning, repenting, worshipping, prostrating to and praising our Lord. Allah was true to His promise: He supported His servant and alone defeated the Confederates.

Also add,

كُلُّ شَيْءٍ هَالِكٌ إِلَّا وَجْهَهُ ، لَهُ الْحُكْمُ وَإِلَيْهِ تُرْجَعُونَ.

Everything is perishing except His countenance [i.e. His essence]. To Him belongs the judgement and to Him you shall return.

When one approaches one's city, it is preferred for one to recite that which has been transmitted when entering any city,

اَللَّهُمَّ إِنِّيْ أَسْأَلُكَ مِنْ خَيْرِ هَـٰذِهِ (أَيْ أَلْبَلَدَةِ) وَخَيْرِ مَا جَمَعْتَ فِيْهَا ، وَأَعُوْذُ بِكَ مِنْ شَرِّهَا وَشَرِّ مَا جَمَعْتَ فِيْهَا. اَللَّهُمَّ ارْزُقْنَا حَيَاهَا وَأَعِذْنَا مِنْ وَبَاهَا. وَحَبِّبْنَا إِلَى أَهْلِهَا وَحَبِّبْ صَالِحِيْ أَهْلِهَا إِلَيْنَا.

O Allah, verily I ask You the best of this (i.e. city), and the best of what You have gathered in it, and I take refuge in You from the worst of it and the worst of what You have gathered in it. O Allah, grant us its prosperity and protect us from its epidemic, make us beloved to its people and make beloved the righteous of its people to us.

When the traveller enters his city, it is recommended that he begins with the mosque if possible; thus he prays two units therein.

It is recommended that one recites when entering one's house,

تَوْباً تَوْباً ، لِرَبِّنَا أَوْباً ، لَا يُغَادِرُ حَوْباً.

Repenting, repenting, to our Lord returning,
who leaves no sin un-erased.

It is also recommended that the pilgrims and travellers are only received from the outskirts of the city, without going too far—if there is no need for that—and the one receiving the pilgrim should ask him to pray for his forgiveness, and those receiving and visiting the pilgrims should supplicate for their good and with what has been related in the hadith,

قَبِلَ اللهُ حَجَّكَ وَغَفَرَ ذَنْبَكَ ، وَأَخْلَفَ نَفَقَتَكَ.

May Allah accept your hajj, forgive your sin and compensate you for what you spent.

The pilgrim in turn should supplicate for the forgiveness and goodness of one's brother or sister, as a pilgrim's prayer is expected to be answered due to the words of the Prophet ﷺ, 'O Allah, forgive the pilgrim and the one for whom the pilgrim seeks forgiveness.'

Concluding remarks

Live, O pilgrim, your remaining life under the shade of your hajj and umrah rituals and their memories and your servitude during them. Furthermore, always encourage people to perform hajj, whether obligatory or voluntary; and likewise the umrah, and arouse in them a longing for that. Beware of what some people fall into in complaining about the congestion and difficulties [during hajj], which discourages people, weakens their resolve and is a barrier to immense good.

Let the impact that hajj or umrah had upon you be a means of increasing your concern for matters related to your religion and dedicating your worldly life (*dunyā*) to achieving the goodness of the Afterlife, for that is the sign of acceptance and a successful pilgrimage.

O Allah, make us amongst those whom You have honoured with an accepted hajj and a rewarded endeavour, and record for us the reward of someone who guides to this great good, and allow us to partake in the rites of the pilgrims, both greater (hajj) and lesser (umrah) and the visitors [of the Prophet ﷺ]: their invocations and supplications. Honour us, O Allah, to return constantly, with ease and attaining acceptance. Enable us, O Allah, to show gratitude for Your blessings and to fulfil their rights well and grant us more of Your immense bounty.

May Allah bless our master Muhammad, his family and his Companions, and give them peace. And may peace be upon the messengers. All praise belongs to the Lord of the Worlds.

Written by the servant of the Qur'an and Hadith and their sciences,

Nūr al-Dīn 'Itr
Faculty of Shariah,
University of Damascus.

Glossary of Arabic Terms and Places

Al-Baqīʿ: the graveyard in Medina situated besides the Prophetic Mosque, wherein many of the renowned Companions, family members of the Prophet ﷺ and Imams, such as Imam Mālik, are buried.

ʿArafah: name of a plain fourteen miles east of Mecca and nine miles from Minā; it is an integral of hajj for pilgrims to be present there on the afternoon of the ninth of Dhū al-Ḥijjah.

Dhū al-Ḥijjah: the last month of the lunar year; it is the month in which the hajj rituals are performed.

Hadith: a report conveying the words, deeds, approval or description of the Prophet ﷺ.

Hadyī: the sacrificial offering from a pilgrim, either as atonement for certain violations committed in hajj, or an expression of gratitude, as in the case of someone performing hajj according to the *al-qirān* or *al-tamattuʿ* methods.

Hajj: the major pilgrimage that comprises various rituals which are to be performed within specific times and at specific locations.

Ḥanafīs: adherents of the school of Imam Abū Ḥanīfah ﷺ (80 –150 AH) from Kufa, founder of one of the four Sunni schools of Islamic jurisprudence.

Ḥanbalīs: adherents of the school of Imam Aḥmad ibn Ḥanbal ﷺ (164 –241 AH) from Baghdad, founder of one of the four Sunni schools of Islamic jurisprudence.

Al-Ḥaram: the Sacred Precinct surrounding Mecca with defined borders, in which hunting game and plucking trees and grass is impermissible; it is also employed to describe the Sacred Mosque in Mecca.

Ḥaṭīm: semi-circular wall around the northern side of the Kaaba, considered to be part of the Kaaba, which is why pilgrims are required to circumambulate around it.

Al-Ḥill: the area in between the *iḥrām* sites and *al-Ḥaram* from where a person in *al-Ḥaram* needs to leave if he wishes to perform umrah.

Ḥijr: synonymous with *Ḥaṭīm* (see *Ḥaṭīm*).

Iḍṭibāʿ: to bare one's right shoulder and cover the left during every *ṭawāf* after which there is *saʿy.*

Al-Ifrād: the sole performance of hajj (i.e. when no umrah precedes it).

Iḥrām: the intention to perform hajj or umrah accompanied by the *talbiyah* according to Ḥanafīs. According to the other Imams it the intention alone.

Istilām: touching the Black Stone, either by kissing and prostrating on it to Allah or, if unable, pointing to it with one's palms opened.

Jamrah (pl. jimār): the (three) sites in Minā that are stoned during hajj; the word is also applied to the stones that are thrown at the sites.

Kaaba: the House of Allah in Mecca, towards which Muslims pray and circumambulate.

Mālikīs: adherents of the school of Imam Mālik ibn Anas رحمه الله (93–179 AH) from Medina, founder of one of the four Sunni schools of Islamic jurisprudence.

Al-Marwah: one of the two mounts adjacent *al-Ḥaram* Mosque in Mecca.

Al-Mashʿar al-Ḥarām: an epithet for al-Muzdalifah or for Mount Quzaḥ therein.

Minā: name of a plain approximately five miles east of Mecca; it is where pilgrims spend the nights from the eighth till the twelfth of Dhū al-Ḥijjah, encamped in tents.

Mīqāt: designated site from which a pilgrim coming from outside it initiates *iḥrām* for hajj or umrah.

Mufrid: a pilgrim performing hajj according to the *al-ifrād* method, which is to perform hajj only (i.e. without an umrah preceding it).

Muḥrim: a pilgrim who has initiated the *iḥrām*.

Multazam: the wall of the Kaaba between its door and the Black Stone.

Mutamattiʿ**:** a pilgrim performing pilgrimage according to the *al-tamattu*ʿ method.

Al-Muzdalifah: name of a valley in between Minā and ʿArafah, which is approximately 1.8 miles from Minā; pilgrims, after spending the day in ʿArafah on the ninth of Dhū al-Ḥijjah, spend the night of Eid therein.

Namirah Mosque: the mosque in ʿArafah where the hajj imam leads the pilgrims in the *ẓuhr* and *ʿaṣr* prayers combined on the Day of ʿArafah (ninth of Dhū al-Ḥijjah).

Qārin: a pilgrim performing hajj according to *al-qirān* method.

Al-Qirān: one of the three methods of performing hajj; it is the performance of umrah and hajj simultaneously with a single *iḥrām*.

Qubā': name of a place on the outskirts of Medina where the first mosque in Islam was built.

Ramal: briskly strutting during *ṭawāf*.

Rawḍah (lit. the 'garden'): the name of an area in between the Prophet's chamber ﷺ and pulpit in his mosque, clearly marked by white pillars.

Saʿ**y:** the walk between the two mounts al-Ṣafā and al-Marwah.

Al-Ṣafā: name of the mount directly parallel to al-Marwah.

Shāfiʿ**īs:** adherents of the school of Imam Muḥammad ibn Idrīs al-Shāfiʿī ﷺ (150-204 AH) from Gaza, founder of one of the four Sunni schools of Islamic Jurisprudence.

Sunnah: the Prophet's way ﷺ and practice; in Islamic legal terms it is an act done by the Prophet ﷺ without him obligating its performance, and if it was done habitually by him ﷺ, it is an emphasised sunnah; otherwise, it is recommended.

Tahlīl: the invocation '*Lā ilāha illa llāh*' (There is no deity except Allah).

Takbīr: the invocation '*Allāhu akbar*' (Allah is the greatest).

Talbiyah: the invocation '*Labbayka Allāhumma labbayk ...*' (Ever at Your service, O Allah, ever at Your service ...), which is recited by a pilgrim during the *iḥrām* for hajj or umrah.

Al-Tamattuʿ: one of the three methods of performing pilgrimage: it is the performance of umrah in the months of hajj followed by the performance of hajj, each with their own respective *iḥrām*.

Al-Tanʿīm: the closest region of *al-Ḥill* to *al-Ḥaram*; pilgrims in Mecca who wish to perform umrah usually depart to it to initiate their *iḥrām*.

Tarwiyah: the name given to the eighth day of Dhū al-Ḥijjah.

Tashrīq: the name given to the three days that follow the Day of Sacrifice: the eleventh, twelfth and thirteenth of Dhū al-Ḥijjah.

Ṭawāf: circumambulation of the Kaaba.

Ṭawāf al-Ifāḍah (lit. the 'Circumambulation of the Departure')**:** it is the obligatory *ṭawāf* in hajj.

Ṭawāf al-Ziyārah (lit. the 'Circumambulation of the Visit'): it is another name for *Ṭawāf al-Ifāḍah*, the obligatory *ṭawāf* in hajj.

Uḥud: a mountain in Medina approximately four kilometres from the Prophet's Mosque ﷺ, wherein the famous battle took place between the Muslims and idolaters in the third year after Hegira, in which seventy of the Prophet's Companions ﷺ, amongst them his uncle Ḥamzah ﷺ, were martyred.

Umrah: the lesser pilgrimage that consists of *ṭawāf* and *saʿy*; it can be performed throughout the year, though offensive on Eid ul-Adha and the four *Days of Tashrīq* following it.

Wādī Muḥassir: name of a valley that separates al-Muzdalifah from Minā.

Zamzam: the name of the famous well in Mecca whose water is blessed.

Ziyarāh: visiting the Prophet ﷺ, his Companions and other historical sites associated with him in Medina.